THE IRISH AND IRISH POLITICIANS

A STUDY
OF CULTURAL
AND SOCIAL
ALIENATION

by Edward M. Levine

THE
IRISH
AND
IRISH
POLITICIANS

UNIVERSITY OF NOTRE DAME PRESS
Notre Dame & London

To the memory of Art Tatum

Acknowledgments

I am indebted to many persons for their contributions to this study, particularly to the politicians, priests, and administrators, chiefly Irish, who were so generous with their time and so remarkably candid in their comments. Without their assistance this book could not have been written. Because they prefer to remain anonymous, my appreciation must be expressed to them in general. (I should add that in all but a few instances, the names used in Chapter 6 are fictitious.) Thanks are also due the citizens of Chicago for making a number of interviews possible through their consistent support of various Irish elective officials.

Especially helpful with their interest, advice, and criticisms were Michael L. Igoe, Jr., and Professor Walter Murphy. Others who read the manuscript in whole or part and who made helpful recommendations are Professors James McRandle, Donald Smithburg, Richard Wade, and Dr. Stephen Barnwell. All have helped improve the quality of this work and were so charitably disposed as to insist upon absolving the writer of the responsibility for such defects as remain.

My thanks also to Dr. Sean O'Heideain, former Consul General of Ireland to Chicago, for the many books on Irish history he made available. And I am truly grateful to Mrs. James Clafee for her concern and able assistance in the early stages of preparation.

I wish to acknowledge appreciation for permission to use quotations from the following publications: *It's the Irish* by Bob Considine; reprinted by permission of Doubleday and Company, Inc. *A History of Ireland* by Edmund Curtis; copyright 1937; reprinted by permission of Barnes and Noble, Inc. *Irish Public Opinion* by Robert M. McDowell; copyright 1944; reprinted by permission of Faber and Faber, Ltd.

Contents

ix

During the Irish uprising of 1916 an Irishman went to confession and told the priest that he had just killed two British soldiers. When the priest did not answer him the Irishman repeated more loudly that he had killed two of the British troops. Still there was no comment from the priest. Feeling very frustrated, the Irishman shouted, "Father, are ye dead?" "Dead I'm not," his confessor replied. "I'm waitin' for you to stop talkin' politics and start confessin' your sins."

Introduction 1

My interest in writing about the Irish and Irish politicians is the result of personal experiences in Chicago during the summer of 1960, when I was administrative assistant to the then newly elected committeeman of the Fifth Ward Regular Democratic Organization. My activities on the local scene, particularly in the intellectual community of which the University of Chicago is the hub, enabled me to become acquainted with many residents of the ward, most of whom were liberals affiliated with either the Independent Voters of Illinois (the local chapter of the Americans for Democratic Action) or the Democratic party.

These individuals had been ardent and very active supporters of Adlai Stevenson in 1952 and 1956, and they were hopeful, if gravely dubious, that he might somehow manage to win the Democratic presidential nomination once again. As an intellectual who conscientiously addressed himself to the critical issues of national and international politics, and as a political figure with an exceptional flair

1

for spontaneous witty expressions, Stevenson had an inordinate appeal to the liberals. The liberals were themselves a well-educated and extremely articulate element
whose interest in the major political questions of the day
was paralleled by their concern about community and
municipal problems. They had enthusiastically and vigorously supported the IVI reform candidate for alderman of
the Fifth Ward and were in fact chiefly responsible for his
having twice defeated the nominees of the previous ward
committeeman.

Characteristic of their political involvement during the
weeks preceding and following the Democratic nominat-
ing convention were the number of activities they initiated,
the emotional intensity and voluble nature of their political
interests, and their eager willingness to serve as part-time
volunteers for precinct work and office chores for both the
IVI and the ward organization. The liberals were manifestly committed to causes.

As a result of my association with the ward organization,
I came to see, meet, and know quite a number of people
working for the committeeman, as well as those associated
with other sectors and levels of the party, including a number of persons holding public office. It soon became evident
that a sizable number of them were Irish, a realization that
was facilitated by the observations of Irish acquaintances,
as well as having been prompted by the flair and tempo of
John F. Kennedy's campaign for the Democratic party's
presidential nomination. Heretofore anonymous "American" names suddenly "became" Irish.

The Irish politicians, in striking contrast to the liberals,
seemed to be a decidedly different type of *homo politicus*.
They were distinguished by a personality and political
style that eschewed flamboyance, rhetoric, repartee, an
ideological orientation, and publicity, in favor of intently
concentrating on the business of the political organization.

Quietly attending to details, the Irish seemed almost absent from the flurry of activities on the local political scene once the election campaign had begun. However, the party's preparations for the presidential and local election campaigns under the leadership of Mayor Richard J. Daley were a constant reminder that the Irish in the party were present, active, and very much accounted for.

The more aware I became of the Irish, the more curious it seemed that so many of them were in urban government and that they found politics so congenial. Politics appeared to suit them as a comfortable and familiar way of life. And quite unlike any of the other immigrant Americans, the Irish were and still are counted in urban politics in the North and East far beyond their proportion of the population. They are also the only ethnic group which has been *identified* with politics, as the term "Irish politician" signifies.

The standard explanation of these phenomena—their having preceded other immigrants to America and having spoken English upon arriving here—seemed somehow unsatisfactory. Why, for example, had the Irish remained in urban politics for generations when, according to the academic literature dealing with the sociological functions of politics, the Irish ought to have abandoned politics for middle-class occupations once it had brought them middle-class status? On the other hand, were the Irish really able to achieve such status? Were they genuinely interested in attaining it? Why had the Irish, in general, remained Democrats for so many decades? And why had they been so eminently successful in remaining in power for so long in the northern and eastern cities?

In endeavoring to answer these questions another, and prior, question came to the fore—the nature of Irish identity. Since it appeared that the cultural values of which it was composed would have affected their involvement in

urban politics both before and during the course of their
acculturation in the United States, it seemed advisable to
ascertain those aspects of Irish identity that most directly
bore on their involvement in politics. Thus it was necessary
to determine the influences most responsible for their development, a task that led to the period in Ireland when
Irish identity, as it was known there and later in America,
was formed.

The next chapter, therefore, gives special emphases to
the many and richly told accounts of Ireland's history,
identifying and bringing out the full significance of the
forces that were decisive in the formation of Irish identity
—the brutal religious persecution, economic destitution,
and political subjugation that Irish Catholics suffered as a
result of the rule of Anglo-Saxon Protestants.

The critical aspect of England's domination of Ireland
was the terrible religious oppression the Irish endured; it
began in full measure with Cromwell's invasion (1649),
reached its climax with the enactment of the Penal Codes
just prior to the end of the seventeenth century, and its
severity did not appreciably diminish until the end of the
eighteenth century. Religious discrimination was ended
only when Ireland won its independence in 1922.

The harsh religious sanctions and the bitter strife they
produced were responsible for the unique and intense commitment of the Irish to Catholicism, for Catholicism's becoming the fundamental cultural value of the Irish, and for
creating the unity of the people, priests, and the Church.
Furthermore, religious persecution was a major reason for
the emergence of the priests and the hierarchy* as the
authoritative voices among the Irish, and partly the reason
for the strongly conservative influence the hierarchy ex-

* The terms priests and clergy refer to those whose authority is
confined to the parish church. The terms hierarchy and prelates refer
to diocesan authorities.

erted then and later in the United States. Indeed, religious conflict is central to understanding the values, identity, and social structure of the Irish and Irish politicians in America, where religious animosity has been the dominant element in their lives for many decades.

The religious dispute also came to justify—and encourage —England's seizure of the vast amount of land it turned over to the many adventurers and colonists it helped settle in Ireland in order to stabilize its control. Thus the Irish were forced out of the most fertile areas and reduced by their conquerors and landlords to a country of peasants who were constantly oppressed by excessive rents, taxes, and tithes, and for whom poverty was a general condition. Because they were so thoroughly and continually exploited, the Irish remained a destitute, illiterate people who had no opportunity to improve their lives while they remained Catholic and sought independence.

Yet their Catholicism was intensified at every turn, particularly by the myriad experiences they had with the many governmental authorities who secured and enforced the interests of Protestant landlords and the English government. The Irish were relentlessly victimized for generations by this invincible power which unhesitatingly and openly employed every devious, corrupt, and punitive practice that would serve the purposes of those it represented. In this setting the Irish became exceptionally knowledgeable about Anglo-Saxon political institutions, processes, and laws, and consummately interested and skilled in the uses of power which had been used against them untempered by considerations of political morality. Thus, except for the English, the Irish were the only immigrant group that came to the United States having any familiarity with Anglo-Saxon government, and they knew it only as a hostile, oppressive force that was a constant presence in their lives.

The cultural mold in which Irish identity was fashioned

was a composite of certain unique and inextricably intertwined religious, economic, and political experiences which
were to shape their destiny for generations after they
settled in America.

Chapter 3 presents a brief account of Ireland's Great
Famine (1847), which resulted in a vast exodus of Irishmen to the United States, particularly into the northern and
eastern cities, and describes the initial experiences of the
Irish in these areas. In addition, this chapter introduces the
contention, developed throughout the remaining chapters,
that the social and economic experiences of these Irish
immigrants were sufficiently akin to those they had known
in Ireland to deprive them, generally, of the opportunity
to assimilate, as well as to inhibit their desire to do so.

Chapter 4 explores these experiences in detail, showing
how the Irish became an alienated people within the larger
society. They found themselves an intensely disliked and
distrusted alien, lower-class, Catholic minority in a middle-
class Protestant society that had inherited and preserved
England's religious animosities and prejudices. The Catholic-Protestant religious cleavage became the emotional
current that sustained Irish identity and solidarity for decades, and the social force responsible for their status as
pariahs.

The social isolation of the Irish was given support and
expression by the Irish clerics' coming to dominate the
Catholic hierarchy, by the social and religious influence of
the parish pastors, and by the parochial school system and
the parish church, which were the institutional symbols of
Irish separatism. The priests, and later the politicians, per-
sonified the immense social distance between the Irish and
Protestant America, a distance that would remain for many
Irish for decades to come.

The alienation of the Irish is also attributable to the
Protestant-led Reform Movement which, apart from its

hostility to Catholics, was socially and ideologically remote from the Catholic Irish, who were generally opposed to its objectives. Thus were the Irish inclined to take a conservative view of national political issues whose proponents were the Protestant Reform Movement, Know-Nothings, and the Republican party.

Unable to enter the dominant society, the Irish kept to themselves and the parish community. Upward social mobility, tantamount to approval of the middle-class Protestants' values and life style, was proscribed for most Irish—particularly for those who, for whatever reasons, could not or did not break away from Irish neighborhoods. Intellectuality was even more suspect to a people who had lost their cultural tradition of centuries past and for whom education was as remote from their lives as it was salient to Anglo-Saxon Protestants.

Given their position in the American social structure, most Irishmen turned to and remained in the Democratic party, the one social institution of consequence that did not spurn or derogate them and through which they entered urban politics. Chapter 5 shows that the Irish turned to government not only because it offered them badly needed jobs, but perhaps as much because it gave them access to political power—which historically had been denied and used against them. Their experiences in Ireland, coupled with those they encountered in the United States, bred in the Irish a pre-eminent, if not exclusive, interest in attaining political power. It also left them with essentially no interest in the advocacy of issues or in questions of social justice, a role they had never known and which was all the more unappealing to them since it was one adopted by Protestant reformers.

The chief interest of the Irish who entered urban politics was, therefore, to secure the party and government positions for themselves and to make of the urban Democratic

parties Irish organizations in which control and party
loyalty were the primary desiderata. And as they won control of the city governments and the parties, they politicized the Irish social structure. For a while, the saloon
was important in this social process, and the police were
always instrumental in it.

Instead of using politics as an avenue to integration in
the middle class, politics enveloped the Irish, and the Irish
social structure became an integral part of the process of
recruiting other Irishmen into both the party and government. As the Irish swarmed into city politics, political office
was recognized as *the* career among them, and politics
became the secular extension of their essentially religious
identity. Political success through the Democratic party
was also the secular equivalent of rising in the hierarchy
of the Catholic Church, in that the most admired figures
among the Irish were usually those who rose to prominence
in each. And, for the most part, it was the Irish who became the power-wielders in these institutions. Still, their
impressive success in politics—and the Church—was also a
mark of their alienation in a society whose views of the
management and ends of government so strongly clashed
with those of the Irish.

Chapter 6 concentrates on the Irish and Irish politicians
in Chicago and seeks to confirm the general analysis of the
preceding chapters.* It examines extensively the influence
of ethnic identity on Irish political behavior by investigating the dominant Irish attitudes affecting political recruitment, political morality, and the Irish political style—all of
which are developments of the dominant religious, class,
and political values that were formed in Ireland and reinforced in the United States. In addition, this chapter dis-
cusses in detail the significance of Catholicism—*Irish* Catholicism—in the lives of the Irish politicians. As will be

* Appendix A describes the interviewing sample and methodology.

seen, this remains the factor most responsible for their diminished, yet still strong, sense of ethnic identity and political solidarity.

None of the material deals with the characteristics so often associated with the Irish—their affability, toughness, humor, wit, or gregariousness. And there is no mention of the numerous individuals responsible for the many and important Irish contributions to American literature and theater, or of the Irish who rose to positions of power in American labor organizations. Neither is there any account of the exploits or careers of particular Irish politicians about whom a good deal has been written.* Nor do the arguments presented claim to hold true for all Irish, especially not for those who lived elsewhere than in the North and East nor for those who upon improving their economic status broke the hold of Ireland's history and acculturated —a trend that began in the later nineteenth century.

Finally, a word about the use of the term "Irish politician." Even though the authority and duties of elected officials differ from those of government administrators and from those who have been party officials without positions in government, all are appropriately referred to as Irish politicians for two reasons. First, they are cut from the same social cloth and have very much the same view of party politics and government, regardless of position. Age is the major differentiating factor, but only because the younger Irish politicians are more socially removed from the ties of Irish communities, of which there are ever fewer traces.

Second, and contingent upon the first, is that Irish poli-

---

* Appendix B includes brief biographical sketches of the social backgrounds and political experiences of Mayor Richard J. Daley and the late Mayor Martin H. Kennelly. The purpose of these accounts is to compare the role of the typical—and transitional—Irish politician (Daley) with the atypical Irish politician (Kennelly).

ticians are, more than any others, *party* politicians; they are deeply engrossed in, well informed about, and seriously attentive to party interests and duties. And where the Democratic party is well organized, as is especially true in Chicago, the Irish are undeviating in their loyalty to the party in all matters of importance. Moreover, the Irish perceive themselves as the only group in the Democratic party whose strength is their primary concern, a view that is, for the most part, accurate.

As the profound social and technological changes of the past several decades have transformed the social character of this society, Irish solidarity and identity have begun to disappear. Ethnic distinctions in general have succumbed to the currents and attractions of assimilation, especially as religious differences are so much less divisive and the general standard of living so vastly improved. Of equal importance for the Irish are the great changes that have occurred within the Catholic Church. Less and less is it "their" Church, just as the Democratic party is less and less "their" party. Simultaneously, the exclusive identities of the Church, the party, and the Irish are fading, and the young Irish politicians are the last of a breed.

The Development
of Irish Identity

2

The unique Irish interest and involvement in city politics, as well as the influence of politics on their outlook and lives, are best understood by turning first to the basic religious, economic, and political events that befell Ireland under England's domination prior to the massive Irish emigration to the United States in 1847-51. The impact of these events transformed Ireland from a land of clans and tribes into a people with a national identity. In addition, these changes led to the emergence of a cohesive Irish social structure and gave rise to the fundamental cultural values upon which it rested.

The incredibly bitter religious conflict that broke out between the Irish Catholics and Anglo-Saxon Protestants, the issue that determined the character of their relationship for several centuries and in terms of which all other major issues ultimately were defined, provides the point of departure of this chapter.

11

RELIGIOUS OPPRESSION: THE REFORMATION, CROMWELL'S CONQUEST, AND THE PENAL CODES

For over a century prior to the Reformation, England had regarded Ireland as an island inhabited by lowly, inferior peasants who, because of England's superior and concentrated forces, might be exploited for the interests of the Crown and for the personal advantage of English adventurers. During this period the English periodically went on plundering forays into Ireland's interior from Dublin, which had been a secured English stronghold since the mid-fifteenth century.

After the Reformation and Henry VIII's break with Rome, however, England changed its policy toward Ireland, deciding that its troublesome Catholic people must at all costs be subdued to eliminate any chance that Ireland might jeopardize England's security. This decision was hastened by the religious strife between English Protestants and Catholics, by the growing religious antagonism between Ireland and England, and by the struggles for the English throne that were as steeped in the acrimony of religious discord as they were due to personal ambitions for power. Another important factor in England's changed attitude toward Ireland was its continuing involvement in continental political struggles with Catholic monarchs who, the English felt, might try to induce the Irish to make war against England when the latter was engaged in hostilities on the Continent.

As for Ireland's reaction to the Reformation, its people had been Catholic for many centuries and were untouched by the causes and consequences of Luther's break with the Roman Church. Irish prelates had not been involved in negotiations with secular rulers for temporal power because Ireland had never experienced any truly serious movement for political unification. There were neither greater nor lesser political stakes involving the authority of the Church in Ireland. Consequently, it had not been tempted by offers of property rights and court preroga- tives in exchange for its acknowledgment of and conces- sions to the growing influence of secular leaders. Untainted by the corruption and venality that led to Luther's stric- tures against and break with the Pope, the Church in Ire- land commanded broad popular support and enjoyed the loyalty of the tribal chiefs.

The first sign that religious hostilities were to dominate Ireland's relationships with England appeared in the ad- vice of the English Council of Ireland to Henry VIII ". . . that he should take the title of King [of Ireland], 'for the Irish have a foolish opinion that the Bishop of Rome is King of Ireland.' "[1] Acting on this suggestion, Henry sought to legitimate his claim as the ultimate authority in both ecclesiastic and secular matters by passing the Act of Su- premacy. This Act sought to compel the Irish hierarchy to recognize Henry VIII as the final authority in matters of faith, a province heretofore the exclusive domain of the Church in Rome. The Irish prelates objected to this in- vasion of their power, and Henry was forced to resort to threats and persecution in order to gain their compliance. As a result,

> . . . sufficient bishops, perhaps a majority, were found to take the Supremacy oath [although the subsequent] change [in their attitude] . . . could only affect Leinster and the nearer areas. Along with [their acknowledgement of Henry] went a policy of anglicization, and bishops and clergy were ex- pected to use and preach in English.[2]

The Act of Supremacy obliged the Irish prelates to deal with the English government and obey it in matters of re- ligion, and outlawed seminaries so that those preparing for the priesthood could obtain training only in seminaries on the Continent chiefly in France. The chief effect of the Act of Supremacy, however, was to politicize the bitter religious discord that became the focal point of the ensuing centuries of conflict between Irish Catholics and Anglo-Saxon Protestants. The religious dispute also provided England with the justification for persecuting the Irish as a means of establishing its power throughout Ireland. These actions preceded its decision to extirpate Catholicism or at least to drive it into the remotest parts of the hinterland, a policy that was established upon the enactment of the Penal Codes.

From the latter part of the sixteenth century onward England continued to extend the area it controlled and increased the severity of its religious sanctions. The Irish who lived under English authority were in some areas compelled to attend Protestant religious services and, when appearing as witnesses and defendants in court, to take oaths on Protestant bibles. While outwardly conforming to this "hated alien faith," the Irish harbored ever greater resentment over such indignities. However distressing were the religious hardships the Irish suffered during this period, these scarcely compared with those inflicted upon them after Cromwell's conquest.

In 1649 Cromwell invaded Ireland in full force and crushed the rebellion that had broken out in 1641 and had spread through the land. The unconditional and harshly penalizing settlement he imposed resulted in the permanent departure of nearly 30,000 officers and soldiers to France and Spain. In addition,

. . . thousands of common Irish were dispatched to the West Indies as practical slaves. The population in the last ten years of war and ravage had fallen to some half mil-

* A description of the Penal Codes and an account of their effects are found on p. 16.

lion, and Ireland was almost a blank sheet on which the English Commonwealth could write what it wished.

. . . .

The amount of land confiscated and planted [was] reckoned by Petty as 11,000,000 (English) acres out of the whole 20,000,000 acres of Ireland, nearly 8,000,000 of these being "profitable." . . . the real result was to create a new landlord class in Ireland; for the adventurers, and also great numbers of army officers, were installed in Irish estates. The Catholic landowners were reduced to a minority and the new English element in the towns never again lost their dominance in the civic and industrial life of the country.[3]

Other restrictive measures imposed after Cromwell's victory barred Catholics from sitting in the Irish Parliament and from holding office in municipal government. In 1672 still other religious sanctions were enacted compelling Catholics to contribute to the upkeep and repair of Protestant churches, and Protestant ministers were authorized to collect fees from the Irish for baptisms and marriages. Priests were permitted to perform these rites only after the fees were paid; the Catholics were, therefore, obliged to pay twice for these ministrations, since the priests depended upon them for their support.

By the end of the seventeenth century the religious issue dominated the relations between the two nations, and

. . . as the cause of the Church and nation became ever more closely identified and the idea of nationality grew up in Europe, the stereotyped division which has lasted till our own time developed. In Ireland the words Catholic and Irishman became almost synonymous, and the word "English" was often used to denote a Protestant.[4]

The most far-reaching and repressive measures devised by England to extirpate Catholicism in Ireland were the Penal Codes, enacted during the period 1692-1727. As if to herald the Penal Codes, the English government in 1691 required the members of both houses of the Irish Parliament "to take an oath of allegiance, a declaration against the Mass, Transubstantiation, and other Roman doctrines, and an oath adjuring the spiritual supremacy of the Pope." Then, unwilling to heed its monarchs who suggested more temperate action, the English Parliament began to pass the Codes, which in a short period of time levelled the remaining social and occupational distinctions among the Irish. Their stringently punitive nature is revealed in the following:

> The Irish were forbidden to: receive education; exercise his religion; enter a profession; hold public office; engage in trade or commerce; live in a corporate town or within five miles thereof; own a horse of greater value than 5 pounds; purchase land; lease land; accept a mortgage on land in security for a loan; vote; keep any arms for his protection; hold a life annuity; buy land from a Protestant; receive a gift of land from a Protestant; inherit land from a Protestant; rent any land worth more than thirty shillings a year; reap from his land any profit exceeding a third of the rent; be a guardian to a child; leave his infant children under Catholic guardianship when dying; attend Catholic worship; and compelled by law to attend Protestant worship. The priest was banned and hunted with bloodhounds. The schoolmaster was banned and hunted with bloodhounds. There sprang up in those days the infamous trade of priest-hunting, "five pounds" being equally the government price for the head of a priest or for the head of a wolf.[5]

The enactment of the Penal Codes marked a turning point in Irish history. Earlier, Cromwell's victory had destroyed the last real vestige of Irish autonomy and, in reducing the Irish to the status of a lowly and subservient people, intensified the religious issue in a way heretofore unknown in Ireland. Now, the Penal Codes officially transformed the religious conflict into the standard that would prescribe the regulations England would henceforth employ to determine the quality of life for the Irish. The Codes literally reduced the conditions of life in Ireland to the lowest possible common denominator.

The Penal Codes were effective in luring some away from the Catholic Church out of want and necessity, and others because they found conversion an expedient means of preserving their property. However, the vast majority of the Irish remained intensely faithful to the Church despite, perhaps because of, the enveloping misery inflicted upon them by the Codes. In fact, the Codes were instrumental in forging the unity of the people, priests, and the Church that became the social foundation of Irish identity and culture.

When the Irish were granted some relief from these sanctions they had already achieved their destructive ends, and the alleviating legislation was no more than a token gesture. As Creel has noted, it was not until 1771 that

> . . . the rare concession was made that allowed Catholics to take a long lease on fifty acres of bog. If it were too deep or marshy to build on, permission was granted to have half an acre of solid land on which to build a home, but with the proviso that the bog should be at least four feet deep and that it should not be nearer than a mile to any market town.[6]

It made little difference that the "purely penal part" of these draconian measures was largely abandoned during the next decade, for they had largely achieved their goal of reducing the Irish to a persecuted people whose standard of living verged on economic servitude.

THE DEVELOPMENT OF A PEASANT ECONOMY

With the advent of the Reformation, England committed itself to the total economic exploitation of Ireland, with

the religious conflict providing it the license to take land at
will. Since Ireland's wealth was in the land, the English
government began

> to root out the Catholic landowners, native and colonist,
> and, insofar as possible, Catholic occupiers, and replace
> them by Protestants from Great Britain. Hence confisca-
> tions and plantations, leading, whenever the opportunity
> arose, to revolt and civil war. Hence an elaborate system
> of penal laws, designed to extirpate Catholic landowners
> and dependence. Hence the establishment of the religious
> ascendancy of a small minority, an institution hardly paral-
> leled in modern times. Hence the tendency to make of
> religion a party badge and emblem, in order to distinguish
> different races and classes. . . .[7]

As its stake in Ireland grew, the English government was
increasingly urged to bring enough colonists to Ireland to
provide sufficient support for its Church and government.
In 1583, when the English were forced to put down a serious uprising by Irish resentment over property losses and
excessive rents charged by the English who had seized
their lands, the Crown's policy became even more stringent.
Now all Ireland was to be colonized to eliminate the necessity for periodically having to quell such uprisings and
contain the general unrest in areas not under its immediate
control. And for over a century whatever disturbances the
English considered rebellions were "followed by confisca-
tion and Plantation." England's military forces drove the
Irish from their property, and English law was used to
legitimate claims to the lands seized from the Irish.

> [The English] had little difficulty in proving the Irish
> mere squatters on "Englishmen's or Crown lands" and so
> dispossess[ed] them or reduc[ed] them to mere leasehold-
> ers or tenants-at-will. According to the English, after 1366
> all of the "mere Irish" living under Brehon [Irish] law were
> "of *Irish and servile condition.*" Even a man of Irish sur-

name, living in a town or manor, might have his right to property or trade questioned.[8]

The first formal economic sanctions were designed to prevent the Irish economy from competing with English enterprises, rather than punitive measures specifically directed at Catholics. The result of these restrictions was the general stifling of economic venture and development throughout Ireland. By 1666 the export of cattle to England had been legally prohibited, depriving the Irish of a large source of income. Another measure forbade Irish merchants to trade with American colonies unless shipments were made in both directions on English ships. English wool manufacturers were able to eliminate competition from Ireland through a regulation which permitted the Irish to ship only the raw product to England's markets. Irish exports of linen to England continued only because England had no linen industry.

The net effect was to prevent any real agricultural and commercial growth or the development of a merchant fleet. Further handicapping Ireland's economic progress was England's seizure of most of the arable lands east and south of the Shannon river following Cromwell's conquest, an action that was accompanied by the forced exodus of much of the Irish population into Connaught, the western, least fertile part of Ireland. Thus, Ireland's economy, particularly among its Catholic population, was kept at the most rudimentary level and was unaffected, because it was bypassed, by the Industrial Revolution. Ireland was converted into an agricultural colony whose essential market function was to serve as a source of raw materials for English manufacturers.

This set of conditions forced Ireland into a stagnant, peasant economy, for its people had no opportunity to learn the skills that were part of the technological and commercial changes occurring in England and on the Continent.

And until they were eased, the Penal Codes required the Irish peasants to divide their land equally among their children, none of whom, therefore, had enough on which to raise sufficient food for a living. Growing numbers of the Irish were forced to become tenant farmers, but even so the rural areas, of which Catholic Ireland was mainly composed, had too little land to support a gradually increasing population. The difficulty was compounded by the inability of the Irish to ease the rural population surplus by sending young people to the towns and cities to find employment, for the latter were almost as economically listless as the hinterland. Ireland's stunted economic (and cultural) development was so pervasive and paralyzing that it has delayed Ireland's urbanizing and industrializing for years after winning independence.

In addition to the formal economic sanctions and land seizures, the Irish had to contend with the exorbitant rents charged by their English landlords for tiny, marginal plots of land upon which they were barely able to eke out a subsistence living. Many of the Irish rented from absentee-landlords residing in England, whose only interest in their property was to make it yield the highest possible return by charging the highest rents the Irish could pay.

Oppressed and frustrated by the rack-rents, the Irish peasants even found themselves penalized for the improvements they made on the land or dwellings they rented, since landlords charged higher rents with each increase in the value of the property. Potter has portrayed this system as follows:

> Landlords did not rent farms in Ireland; they rented land. The tenant had to provide for himself, make his own repairs, care for his own fencing and drains; build his own outbuildings, undertake his own improvements, and use his own implements; and his reward was either a higher rent because of the improvements wrought by his sole

capital—his own muscles—or an ouster to make room for a man ("the grabber") who would pay a higher rent.[9]

This system not only effectively discouraged individual initiative and destroyed the tenants' hopes of ever attaining a better life through their own efforts, it also began to aggravate their discontent over these unjust practices from which they had no relief. Out of such conditions emerged

. . . a mortal struggle for existence between the cotters on the one side and the "middlemen" and the tithe-proctors on the other . . . and a century of agrarian conspiracy and crime was the result.

It was under conditions like these that the suspicion of the law and its ministers became worked into the very nerves and blood of the Irish peasant. His lawlessness, which scarcely exceeded the lawlessness of the landlords' magistrates who rule[d] him, was not political, but directed against the land system and the tithe system from which he suffered.[10]

The few who owned land fared little better than those who rented, for they had only enough land for a marginal existence. Their pieces of land were unproductive despite the best care, because the soil was so poor and because none could afford to invest in better seed for hardier and more productive crops. The Irish typically lived a hand-to-mouth existence on the plainest, and usually meatless, fare. Those who owned land held onto it as long as they were able to farm it, not passing it along to the eldest son until he was well along in years. The rest of the children had no alternative to becoming tenant farmers, since they had no land inheritance or opportunities for employment in the towns and cities. Consequently, the number of those who became tenant farmers, frequently in vicious competition with each other for tiny plots of land, increased until they comprised the bulk of the populace.

... poverty was deep and widespread. A member of parliament ... once declared that, "this island is supposed to contain three millions, of these two millions live like beasts of
the field upon a root picked out of the earth." ... The peasants were denoted "our aborigines" and compared to the
wildest of Indians for cruelty and lawlessness. They were
described as having for clothing one frieze coat and one
bandle shirt, and living on a staple diet of potatoes, milk
and salt, and it was said that round the southern sea coast
the lower orders could not afford to purchase milk, so that
potatoes and herrings were their only support. As for the
hovels in which the peasants lived their condition can be
inferred from an argument used against the window tax. It
was no use imposing such a tax since the poor had no win-
dows on which to pay it. Their cabins were described by a
young Englishman who visited Ireland at the end of the
eighteenth century, as being six to seven feet high, having
for their floor soil, and for a door a bundle of furze, with the
pig as a "parlour boarder." ... if a person had never visited
Ireland he could have no conception of the deplorable conditions of the lower orders.[11]

Such was the desperate plight of the Irish masses who,
from the middle of the seventeenth century onward, were
socially, economically, and politically devastated. It was
not until the 1830's that efforts of Irish political agitators
were able to win slight and temporary relief from England
for the economic distress suffered in all parts of the land.

THE EMERGENCE OF IRISH SPOKESMEN: THE PRIESTS AND THE HIERARCHY

England realized that the success of its rule in Ireland
was greatly dependent upon the elimination of its chief
opposition, the Irish hierarchy. Insofar as the Church maintained its sovereignty in ecclesiastical matters, it remained

the institutional symbol of Irish identity and so the ultimate source of Irish resistance to England. Therefore, when the Church survived the Oath of Supremacy despite the coercive measures taken against its prelates, the English government realized that the priests' influence with the people must be eradicated to destroy the link between the people and Catholicism. Thus the English singled out the "priests as the personification of that powerful combination of political and religious resistance to English rule which was . . . to become basic in Irish nationalism."[12] The enactment of the Penal Codes provided the English with all conceivable means to rid Ireland of its priests. *

Despite the stringent interdictions of the Penal Codes and of other statutes enacted later, the priests continued to celebrate the Mass knowing that to do so meant to jeopardize their lives. Masses were held clandestinely, after dark in forest clearings, in the fields, in cottages, in barns— wherever it was possible to gather the Irish peasants together secretly. Despite their extreme efforts, the English failed to destroy the faith of the priests and the people or to weaken their commitment to Catholicism. Instead, they created an unbreakable bond between the priests and the people by forcing them into the same set of oppressive circumstances.

The priests' living conditions were identical with those of their parishioners, upon whom they were completely dependent for their sustenance. It was both common and

---

* Even in the latter part of the eighteenth century the English sought to eliminate the priests by controlling their religious functions. They offered "an annuity to every priest who would forsake his creed, pronounced a sentence of exile against the whole hierarchy, and restricted the right of celebrating Mass to registered priests, whose number, according to the first intention of the legislature, was not to be renewed." W. Lecky, "History of Ireland in the Eighteenth Century," in James Carty, ed., *Ireland: 1783-1850* (Dublin: C. J. Fallon, 1949), p. 101.

necessary for priests to seek food and lodging from peasant families, moving each day or so to lighten the burden of assistance that none could assume for more than a very short period. In this way the priests intimately shared both the meager existence and the unrelieved adversity of those upon whom they depended and to whom they ministered. In turn, they were able to offer their parishioners spiritual comfort, the helpful explanation and solace for the abject misery of their everyday lives. The closeness and importance of the priests to the people was commented on by Gustave de Beaumont after his visit to Ireland.

> Survey these immense lower classes in Ireland who bear at once all the charges and miseries of society, oppressed by the landlord, exhausted by taxation, plundered by the Protestant minister, their ruin consummated by the agents of law. Who or what is their only support in such suffering?—The priest—Who is it that bestows on them, what is perhaps more precious, that consoling sympathy, that sustaining voice of sympathy, that tear of humanity, so dear to the unfortunate? There is but one man in Ireland that mourns with the poor man who has so much to mourn, and that man is the priest. . . . In Ireland the priest is the only person in perpetual relation with the people who is honoured by them.[13]

The clergy were frequently very active in secular affairs, by which they were more often than not as directly affected as their parishioners. As those who had been most exposed to the religious sanctions of the Penal Codes and as the immediate standard-bearers, mediators, and symbols of the dogma, institutions, and traditions of the Catholic Church, the clergy developed enormous prestige among the people. Thus, when the Irish revolted in 1798, priests appeared as the leaders of the Irish peasants in their skirmishes and pitched battles with the Protestants. Their authority as men of the Church and their personal involvement with their parishioners' hardships made them the natural leaders of various insurrectionary groups during those times. "Great numbers of rebels acknowledged no other leader than Father John Murphy . . . who raised the flag of insurrection in the county of Wexford."[14]

By now the priests enjoyed a preeminent status among the people, and since Ireland had no other voices to provide leadership and counsel,

> the priest became everything—aristocrat, intellectual, and spiritual director all in one. . . . Irish priests were supposed to stay out of the "troubles," but they never did. They were loyal to the Vatican generally, however, though they regarded the Italian people as a pagan lot who thought they could skip Mass because they were "the Pope's cousins."[15]

The priests' involvement in politics was to be of special importance a generation later when the Catholic Association* was formed. In addition, their authority in secular matters was to have an influential bearing on the destinies of those they joined in America.

In contrast with the priests, the Irish hierarchy was remote from the people and their troubles. Aware that its existence depended upon the sufferance of England, the hierarchy sought only to win accommodations that would assure its survival and thus consistently refrained from openly identifying with or supporting the periodic uprisings of the people. Its position became even more conservative as a result of events that occurred in the last decade of the eighteenth century.

In 1798 the Irish revolted as a result of popular discontent over tithe exactions and rack-rents, religious persecution, and the great appeal of the French Revolution. This rebellion, in conjunction with the grave concern in England

* See p. 42.

over the excesses and goals of the French Revolution, abruptly halted the English Parliament's slight interest in alleviating conditions in Ireland. In its opposition to the French Revolution and its fear of the contagious effects the Revolution seemed likely to have in Ireland, England gained a curious ally in Ireland's Catholic Church. In this instance the Church took its cues from Rome and sought to stabilize its position by cooperating with the English government. Curtis, among other writers, has argued that "the Roman Church was the friend of Monarchy and Religion and a great bulwark against revolution and atheism. Its bishops, priests, and respectable classes in Ireland expressed unfeigned horror of the French Republic."[16]

Both the French and American Revolutions had encouraged the Irish to believe that they might somehow free themselves from England. The Irish hierarchy, however, was alarmed by the French Revolution, which was directed as much against the Church as the monarchy. If the "rights of man" and "reason" were the foundations of a political movement to overthrow the established order of both Church and state, then liberty, equality, and fraternity were necessarily suspect by the Irish prelates, who felt compelled to condemn the Revolution and to warn the Irish against its dangers.

The Irish Protestants (dissenters of various Protestant denominations, not Anglicans) were also heartened by the objectives of the French Revolution. Although they opposed the Jacobins' atheism and were disturbed by the emphasis it received, they felt that it was essentially a reaction against the Roman Catholic Church. On the other hand, they were enthusiastic adherents of political equality and as anxious as the Irish Catholics to rid themselves of England's domination of Ireland's economy. Their support of the political doctrines of the Revolution was an additional and important reason for the refusal of the Irish hierarchy to permit Irish Catholics to support this movement. The power of the Church over the Irish, even those who resented clerical interference in so obviously a secular realm, was final.

On the whole, Irish radicalism, while strongly tinctured with anti-clericalism, and in the case of some individuals affected by the current philosophical heterodoxies, seems to have despised and repudiated Paine's theological efforts. Still the reputation of Paine the atheist was a heavy liability to the followers of Paine the politician, and conservatives already horrified by the excesses committed against religion in the course of the French revolution, had yet another reason for associating innovation in politics with infidelity in religion.[17]

With the outbreak of the French Revolution and the political and doctrinal threats it posed to Catholicism, the Catholic Church in Ireland conclusively established itself among the Irish as the sole authority to determine the Catholic view on ideological issues affecting the fundamental interests of the Church. Apart from its ecclesiastical authority, the Irish Church had won the respect of the people by having withstood the onslaught of the Penal Codes. Perhaps of even greater importance, however, was that the Irish Church was the only institution that symbolized the spiritual values and the hopes, however faint, of the Irish. Furthermore, as Protestantism remained the force responsible for their misery, the Irish reflexively turned to the Church when it spoke on doctrinal matters. On unmistakably critical issues they invariably heeded its bidding, if with occasional reluctance. Consequently, any political movement that was imputed to have an atheistic or Protestant influence would henceforth draw the Irish hierarchy's condemnation and the aversion of the Irish.

The Irish hierarchy's action was negative as well as defensive, for it chose not to suggest or articulate a social philosophy that was compatible with the Church's interests and functional for the needs of the Irish peasantry. It also failed to draw the popular interest in democracy under its authoritative tutelage, and thus was identified as an intransigent defender of the status quo and a staunch advocate of political conservatism.

As religion and politics became ever increasingly intertwined through the priests' active involvement with the people and the hierarchy's political promulgations, a parallel development occurred among the people. The Irish had formed secret associations* to strike back at the landlords in retaliation for the crushing rents and taxes they had to bear. Through these associations, some of which had existed for a number of years, the issues of religious and economic oppression were given a scattered, popular base that accentuated the angry, restive mood of the times.

The years that spawned the Revolution of 1798 marked the first time during England's domination of Ireland that popular groups conducted such widespread retaliatory actions. As the situation in Ireland grew worse, these associations defiantly identified themselves and fought their battles in terms of the religious conflict, with the result that the uprising of 1798 became as much a religious civil war as a revolt of people who could no longer endure economic hardships. The religious issue was so intensified during these turbulent times that new symbols emerged to identify the religious adversaries; the Catholics were now identified as the "Green," and the Protestants as the "Orange." The hapless plight of the former is expressed in the tune they sang, "The Wearing of the Green."

> "O Patrick dear! and did you hear
> The news that's going round?
> The shamrock is by law forbid
> To grow on Irish ground.

* See p. 40.

No more St. Patrick's day we'll keep—
His color can't be seen,
For there's a bloody law agen
The wearing of the Green."

The more militant Protestants in northern Ireland, the Orange-men, expressed their enmity toward the Irish Catholics when they raised their cups to the "full Orange toast:"

To the Glorious, Pious and Immortal memory of the great and good King William, who freed us from Pope and Popery, Knavery and Slavery, Brass Money and Wooden Shoes, and he who refuses this toast may be damned, crammed, and rammed down the Great Gun of Athlone.

To this day Orange and Protestant are synonymous and hated terms among many Catholics in Ireland, and there are more than a few Irish Catholics in the United States who do not look upon them kindly.

The Catholic Church was adamantly opposed to all the secret associations and their use of force. It advocated "moral force, patience, and perseverance, and keeping within the law" as the proper means for ameliorating Ireland's duress. It has been argued by some that the Church's interdiction of these groups was due to the secret oaths required of the members of these associations, which the prelates judged to be in conflict with the unconditional fidelity demanded by the Church. It seems more realistic to regard the Church's dictum as prompted by its fear that the rebellious actions of these groups would drive the English government to more repressive statutes or revive old ones.

The deeper significance of the Church's position is that it deliberately refused to support or assist these organizations by recommending that they use their energies constructively—however gradual and restrained their pursuits would necessarily have been. The Church closed off all alternatives to the violence which their overflowing frustrations and anger incited them until Ireland won its independence. In proscribing such groups the Church bypassed the opportunity to facilitate the development of a popular and clerical interest in a political dialogue that might have begun to create effective public support for political organizations and political change. In deterring and decrying the activities of groups committed to social change, the Church could only futilely criticize the illegal activities for which it was at least partly responsible.

The Church remained unmovably conservative through all the political troubles that befell Ireland. It was unwilling to address itself to or encourage popular interest in issues of social and economic reform that the Irish might have used as a basis for political organization and action, and it persistently discouraged those who openly argued, wrote, or fought for such ends. Its outlook remained unchanged in the 1840's, when political liberalism strove to overturn European monarchies and weaken the political and social power of the Church. The Irish hierarchy was especially hostile to the Irish radicals who "advocated international republicanism, in the spirit of European rationalism and enlightenment." Commenting on the reasons for the failure of the Irish uprising in 1848, Dennis Gwynn wrote with misgivings about the influence of the hierarchy:

> Much has been said by party writers about the disloyalty of the Catholic Clergy, but it is my sincere belief that it was through the instrumentality of the superior order of the Catholic Clergy that the insurrection was suppressed. For my own part, I feel convinced that we were defeated, not by the military preparations of Lord Harding or of General MacDonald, but by the influences brought into action by the Catholic Clergy. Whatever merit therefore is connected with the repression of our effort is due chiefly, if not solely, to the Catholic Hierarchy.[18]

The more detached view of Gladstone, who wrote later in the nineteenth century, confirms the observation of Gwynn and others who regarded the Church as insistent in its opposition to indigenous activist movements seeking to improve conditions in Ireland. Gladstone observed:

> . . . I look at the Roman Catholic majority, but I cannot treat the Roman Catholic majority of that period as being entirely one. It is quite clear that both the Roman Catholic aristocracy and prelates stood in a position distinct from the mass of the Roman Catholic people, and were liable to act on inducements held out to them from this side of the water.[19]

By its deliberate inaction the hierarchy failed to provide a moral foundation in terms of which the Irish could have justified their right to relief from the oppression they bore, as well as the right to organize for ameliorating their conditions. Thus the hierarchy created by default a moral vacuum for Irish political affairs, a void that, as will be seen later in this chapter, was filled by distinctive Irish attitudes toward the acquisition and uses of power rather than by ethical principles.

THE POLITICIZATION OF THE IRISH

By the beginning of the seventeenth century England had increased its sphere of influence in Ireland, with the Pale having more than doubled in size and the counties of Connacht, Clare, and Munster having come under its control. To safeguard against disorder in these areas, English authority was more extensively secured and Ireland's new political structure took form.

> [At this time] a new order had begun and . . . all Ireland was to be united as a kingdom under an English monarchy.

The whole country was for the first time shired, and English sheriffs, justices on assize, juries, and all the other forms of English law, land-tenure, and local administration appeared everywhere. Sir John Davies . . . through the country enforced for the first time the Common law and inquired into the principles of the Brehon code and the Irish system of land-tenure which was now swept away and replaced by the ordinary rules of English landlordism.[20]

English government was set up, at least in the person of law enforcement officials, in most parts of Ireland during the remainder of the seventeenth century, particularly after Cromwell undertook to establish England's rule throughout the land. Nevertheless, despite the great anger the Irish felt over their loss of autonomy and so much of their land, the dire political consequences of English rule became evident to them only with the enactment of the Penal Codes. The Codes

. . . excluded the Catholics from the [Irish] Parliament, from the magistracy, from the corporations, from the university, from the bench, and from the bar, from the right of voting at parliamentary elections or at vestries, of acting as constables, as sheriffs, as jurymen, of serving in the army or navy, of becoming solicitors, or even holding the position of gamekeeper or watchman. They prohibited them from becoming schoolmasters, ushers, or private tutors. . . .[21]

When the effects of these restrictive measures are combined with the Codes' religious and economic sanctions, it is evident how degraded life had become in Ireland. And in the midst of their destitution, Irish tenants who were unable to meet their rent payments were summarily evicted by the law enforcement authorities carrying out the edicts of the landlords. The role of government officials in eviction proceedings is described by Potter in the following:

After legal notice of dispossession had been served on the tenants for a set date, the sheriff, or an assistant, arrived at the head of a body of uniformed troops and police, to exercise force if eviction met with resistance. The ejected stood around in groups by their dislodged, pathetic household articles, the men bursting with impotent rage, the women wailing and weeping, the children with bewildered and frightened faces, trying to help the aged, and the dispossessed bed-ridden were exposed to God knows what future. . . . A crowd of laborers, often paupers brought from afar, either deroofed the cabin by firing the thatch or leveled it to the ground, to make it uninhabitable against the later crawling back by the evicted. The soldiers and police then regimented the evicted from the estate itself and left them huddled on the road. . . .[22]

The Irish were so entirely caught up in a web of restrictions and regulations that government officials were an omnipresence in their routine existence. Such small savings as the Irish peasants had managed to put aside by doing extra work at home or as off-season laborers on English farms was not clear gain; when they took their produce to town they paid a toll on each item since the town was the property of the landlord. Furthermore, the Irish were subject to a county rate that was determined by grand juries composed of landlords who used their authority to assure the repair of roads near their estates.

The whole of the eighteenth century was a period of frustration born of a wretched existence from which there was no escape. Each decade was but another measure of time whose hardships were no more than a reliving of the past, a continuation of scarcity and oppression. Agrarian uprisings broke out everywhere during the century, and lawlessness became the general condition. Hoping to force concessions from the Protestant landowners, as well as eager for revenge, the Irish destroyed their property and killed their hirelings. The impersonal, unfeeling law, which had been used as an instrument of subjugation and deprivation and had failed to preserve order, was universally despised by the Irish.

The Irishman who willingly shared his last potato with a beggar would murder, or conspire to murder, a man who tried to take his land, without the slightest pity for the victim or remorse for the dead.

. . . .

The Catholic Irish had no trust in the law or administration of justice. The Rev. William O'Brien, a pastor in County Cork, put the case simply and bluntly: "If you tell an Irishman that he will receive justice in a court of justice no matter what your religion is, he will not believe you." The lower orders . . . [were] "of the opinion that the laws were not made for their protection; they know no parts of them *except the penal and punishing parts.*"[23]

While the Irish had acquired a deep respect for power itself, they had come to detest the symbols and possessors of power. Locally, where the pressure of government was ever visible and frequently encountered, the police were special objects of popular derision. The account below, from the early 1800's, illustrates the utter disrepute in which the Irish held the law and its officials.

Some hundreds of police, with rifles and fowling pieces, were drafted into Dundalk where [a] trial was heard. They were invading troops in a hostile country, rigidly boycotted by all inhabitants of the town whom they had come "to protect from intimidation." Outcasts and pariahs, food, drink, and every form of accommodation was refused them.

On the other hand, the "criminals" were honoured guests, feted and cheered by the entire population.[24]

Irish political morality was both directly opposed to that of the English, as well as the latter's logical counterpart.

The Law: Justice vs. Interest

The bias and ruthlessness of Anglo-Saxon law and the indifference of English magistrates to Irish interests were insurmountable obstacles to any hopes the latter had of obtaining justice. It was thoroughly unrealistic for them to expect the courts to render decisions against the landlords. On the other hand, in cases where both litigants were Irish, a frequent enough occasion, law was an irrelevancy in the face of contradictory claims when each pressed for a biased judgment at the expense of objective justice. The penurious Irish had no use for careful legal analysis and dispassionate judicial decisions; each wanted the law to favor his cause—in the same way it supported the landlords against the Irish. The Irish were compelled by the nature of the legal system to *bargain* for justice and forced to resort to illegitimate means to gain some consideration for their claims. Otherwise, justice was predetermined. As a result of their experiences with the courts the Irish had seen

> . . . that matters went by favor rather than by right. . . . This they called "interest." . . . the Irish peasant believed that "unless he ha[d] what they called interest, he ha[d] no chance of success before any tribunal.

If a man became entangled with the law, his relatives and friends immediately set in motion the machinery of "interest," beseeching the landlord, the agent, the politician, the priest, everyone they believed had power and influence, to put in a "word" for Pat or Owen. A magistrate rarely blinked his eyes in surprise if he found himself showered with gifts of fowl and eggs from relatives and friends of a man soon to stand trial. One of the benefits of belonging to a strong faction was that it frequently enjoyed the protection of its "interest" by a magistrate. In return, the magistrate expected the free labor of the faction in digging, planting and harvesting. A magistrate who set himself out for "interest" was apparently no less respected for his susceptibilities. The people had more faith in the "interest" of a partisan magistrate than they had in the law of the land. They had more trust in the personality of a human being than in the impersonal workings of the law.[25]

Since judicial decisions were most often determined by negotiations based upon favors and influence, trickery, cunning, bribery, and personal contacts became the standard techniques of obtaining "justice." In ordinary cases of litigation, an informal, highly personalized system of law replaced the formal, completely impersonal one. Not only did the exchange of favors and skirting the law become the customary procedures for negotiating with the authorities for favorable decisions, but the Irish regarded them as legitimate since they were the only means which effectively served their interests. Only illegal or devious methods availed the Irish of the justice they considered their due. For an Irishman to proceed through formal channels, placing himself at the mercy of the authorities and the law, was naively, perhaps stupidly, to restrict himself to the norms of a legal system in which personal intervention had no place and from which little justice and no mercy could be expected. The Anglo-Saxon political "morality" that supported countless instances of injustice and legal severity taught the Irish that a countervailing political code was necessary if the stringent laws were to be made more reasonable, the stern justices of the peace and the landlords more accommodating.

Toward the end of the eighteenth century the Protestant landowners acquainted the Irish with new corrupt political practices. Following Ireland's decades-old agitation for the right to vote in local elections, England, in 1793, extended the franchise to those Irish Catholics who were forty shilling freeholders.[26] The use to which this vote might be put was immediately apparent to the English (and the Irish),

who promptly exerted economic sanctions to prevent the
Irish from freely exercising the vote.

> . . . the bestowal of the franchise on Catholics by the Irish
> [Protestant] Parliament . . . had established in Ireland a
> near approach to household suffrage. The right to vote
> was given by a freehold of 40s., this consisting, in the great
> majority of cases of a lease for life. The great landholders
> . . . vied with each other in the creation of these free-
> holds. On election days these tenants were brought to the
> poll by the driver of the estate, like so much live stock
> conveyed to a market. The oath as to the value of the
> freehold was tendered with the same prompt indifference
> as the vote.[27]

Casting a vote (there were no secret ballots) against
the landlord's candidate (frequently the landlord himself)
often led to the eviction of tenants who had become freeholders. Many of them, however, had attained this status
by the open contrivance of the landlords who openly com-
peted with each other in creating freeholds to assure themselves of election to office. Such undisguised political
machinations thoroughly acquainted the Irish with the
art of manipulating the vote.

Reacting as much to the issue of religious discrimination
as in anger over the meaningless franchise given their
parishioners by deceitful landowners, the priests vigorously
condemned the fraudulence of these elections. Aware of
their influence over the people, the landowners accused the
priests of intimidating their parishioners by threatening the
refusal of the sacrament to those who obeyed the voting
instructions of their landlords. The landlords' protest was
both correct and futile, for the priests sternly rebuked those
who had yielded to the landlords and warned others
against such dereliction.

> "If there be a Catholic elector of this borough," said the
> Reverened John Maine, addressing a meeting at Tralee,

"who will dare to go forward and register his vote for an English enemy, pass him by with scorn and contempt; do not be seen to walk with him, to talk with him, or associate with him. Let him fester in his corruption; be not you contaminated by any contact with a wretch so base and degraded. Despise him; if you meet with him on the highroad, pass over to the other side. Have no dealing with him. Make him to understand that he cannot afford to brave the honest indignation of his fellow-countrymen."[28]

English political chicanery and connivance at the local level had its national counterpart, with the result that there was nowhere a standard of political morality acting as a positive influence on individuals who were in control of local government offices. In effecting the union of the Irish and English Parliaments (1800), which eliminated the little self-government Ireland had enjoyed, England had so liberally and blatantly exchanged money, offices, and titles as to move Henry Grattan (an Irish Protestant) dejectedly to comment:

> From the bad terms which attend the Union, I am naturally led to the foul means by which it has been obtained—dismissals from office, perversion of the place bill, sale of peerage, purchase of boroughs, appointment of sheriffs with a view to prevent meetings of freemen and freeholders, for the purpose of expressing their opinion on the subject of a Legislative union—in short the most avowed corruption, threats, stratagems, accompanied by martial law to deprive a nation of her liberty.[29]

In the late eighteenth and early nineteenth centuries Ireland's towns and villages expanded as a result of the increase in population. The growth of these communities provided the Protestant elite with the occasion to establish local governments over which they were careful to maintain complete control. The means by which they retained their monopoly of power is summarized by McDowell:

Each corporation was composed of a governing body, together in some cases with freemen. Except in the case of Dublin the members of the governing bodies were self-elected. Where they were not, matters were so arranged that the governing body exercised considerable influence over the elections. The electors—where there were elections—were the freemen, and the freemen were usually admitted by the governing body. Though Catholics had been eligible for membership since 1793, the corporations were in 1834, with one exception, exclusively Protestant bodies. Except in a few towns the corporate revenues were small, having suffered from mismanagement and fraud, and frequently a considerable proportion was absorbed in the salaries of their higher officers. Though most of the corporations had a staff of decoratively designed and poorly paid officials, they performed few useful functions.[30]

The sum of their experiences with government led the Irish to define politics as an incessant struggle between those in authority and those who had none. The former would inevitably use the power of government to satisfy their interests at the expense of those over whom they held it. Since the Irish were everywhere suppressed by the law and its officials, those Irishmen who assisted the English (and there were more than a few) were regarded as having deserted the Catholic Irish for the Protestant English, and guilty of a traitorous act. This feeling toward those who curried favor with the "enemy" was the basis for the oaths of absolute loyalty and silence that were stringently imposed by the secret societies,* but which were also generally honored by the Irish.

The importance of loyalty was so widely and keenly felt that it found its way into nineteenth- and twentieth-century Irish novels, which treat it as a natural aspect of the social landscape. The following excerpts from Anna Maria Hall's short stories, "Going To Law" and "Do You

Think I'd Inform," point up the contempt in which the
Irish held the law and the baseness of informing on one's
own kind.

It isn't *Law,* please yer honour, only a question. Sure it
isn't the likes o' me would be trying to get law out of yer
honour without paying for it.

.   .   .   .

I'll tell them . . . when they see a prosperous man reduced to begging and forced into exile, I'll tell them *that's
what he got by going to law.*[31]

The following are taken from the second story.

. . . there is something very mean in an *informer.*

.   .   .   .

Do you think I'd inform? No one belonging to me ever
turned informer.

.   .   .   .

. . . Irish assistance is much more easily procured *against*
the law THAN FOR IT.[32]

Irish Action Organizations

The secret associations that sprang up throughout Ireland
in the eighteenth century shared the general desire to
strike back at the landlords and the authorities. Some were
formed with the unfounded hope of successfully fomenting
insurrection, others with the purpose of using any means of
violence to take reprisals against the landowners and the
police. Their members were angry, desperate men who
murdered men and maimed cattle without remorse. During
the Revolution of 1798 both they and the Orangemen in
Ulster were guilty of such inhumane acts as setting fire to
barns into which innocent men, women, and children had
been forced.

Later, in the 1830's, a ferocious struggle broke out when

the secret societies organized militant resistance to the tithes. The power of the Whiteboys during this period was said "to surpass Dublin Castle in vigour, promptitude, and efficacy, so that it was more safe to violate the law than to obey it." Still, these groups fought no "wars," won no "battles," and gained few meaningful concessions from the landowners and the government. More than anything else they symbolized the rage and frustration of an oppressed people.

Despite their general ineffectiveness except as a means of venting pent-up rage, the secret associations schooled the Irish in certain phases of politics. For example, they introduced their members to organizations that made absolute claims on their loyalty, accustomed them to taking orders without question from strong-willed leaders, and acquainted them with the tactics of local operations and with the organizational structure upon which these operations were so very dependent.

Because they were illegal organizations, their very existence and the nature of their guerrilla activities demanded more than mere loyalty to faction or group. Those who joined took an oath which forbade them both to drop their membership in the societies and to reveal any information about their activities. These men were also committed to "declare" themselves, to "stand up" for the principle or interest valued by the groups to which they belonged. This type of commitment, which became ingrained in Irish culture, has been portrayed by William Carleton in one of his stories about Irish villagers. Reminiscing about his youth, he wrote:

> A species of ambition prevails in the Green Isle not known in any other country. It is an ambition of about 3 miles by 4 in extent—or in other words, is bounded by the limits of the parish in which the subject of it may reside. In my own case its first development was noticed in the

hedge-school which I attended. I had not been there long till I was forced to declare myself either for the Caseys or for the Murphys, two tiny factions that had split the school among them.[33]

Even though many of these secret groups were spontaneously formed and clandestinely maintained, they introduced the Irish to a wealth of experience in devious "political" practices which, in view of the Machiavellian political climate, necessarily were unaffected by moral considerations.

The Catholic Association

Following the Napoleonic Wars Irish political activists pressed Britain for the improvement of conditions in Ireland. They were first of all united in their interest to remove the prohibition against Irish Catholic representation in the British Parliament. They were also urged on by the exaction of tithes from the Irish Catholics for the Protestant Establishment in Ireland and by a severe famine that struck the country in 1822. Further provocation resulted from the suspension of the Habeas Corpus Act and a special invoking of the Insurrection Act as a result of new outbreaks of "robbery, murder, and assassination," which once again were the Irish way of responding to their traditional grievances—rack-rents, hunger, and religious persecution. The combined pressure of all these incidents brought about the formation of the Catholic Association in 1823.

The Catholic Association was led by Daniel O'Connell, who had gained national attention as the leading figure in the movement to achieve religious equality for Catholic Ireland. O'Connell and several of his friends created the new organization, whose very carefully stated purpose was "to adopt all such legal and constitutional measures as may be most useful to obtain Catholic Emancipation." The collaborators were obliged to resort to vague language to prevent England from outlawing the Association by invoking the Convention Act (1796), which stipulated that all groups in Ireland appointed by delegation or having any representative character were unlawful. To comply with the law, O'Connell and his friends opened membership in the Association without religious qualifications and declared it to be a body having neither representatives nor delegates.

At the outset the Catholic Association was little more than a debating club. Within a few months of its formation, however, the Association began to receive small donations from people in all parts of the island and had gained the enthusiastic support of the clergy. Still, it had not yet inspired active participation, and several of its meetings were adjourned for want of a quorum. With the hope of providing the necessary momentum for the Association, O'Connell made an open appeal for public support.

> Let the people be appealed to, he suggested: let subscriptions be invited in every town, in every village.
>
> Collectors should be appointed for each parish to receive the monthly subscriptions, the lowest being fixed at a penny, the highest at 2s. In this way the peasant, the workman, the small tradesman, would feel that he had a voice in the association—that he was working in the common cause. [The plan] succeeded marvelously. Collectors volunteered in every part of Ireland.
>
> . . . .
>
> The institution of the Catholic Rent, so the subscriptions were called, stimulated discussion from one end of Ireland to the other.[34]

The people responded eagerly to his request for their help, certain that at last an organization was genuinely concerned with their problems. Indeed, until the Association there had never been an Irish Catholic organization of any significance, let alone one that was national in scope. The Association's appeal to the people was all the more irresistible by having united the political and religious leaders who appeared to be ready to take concerted action on behalf of all Ireland. The Association also marked the first occasion since England had conquered Ireland that political leaders, priests, and the people were actively and effectively collaborating for common purposes. Political leaders had now won a measure of prominence among the people, and politics and religion were joined in interest, organization, and action:

> [The Catholic Association had] a committee . . . formed in every barony of the county [of Waterford]; each had its local agents, with a precise registry accounting for every voter in every parish. On Sunday, members were deputed to address the villagers from the altar steps.
>
> .   .   .   .
>
> The chapel had become purely and simply the village club, holding meetings in a cause none the less sacred because it was human.[35]

Initially the Association was exposed to great ridicule because of its "penny-a-month plan for liberating Ireland." Its critics failed to recognize that conditions were opportune for such a scheme to succeed, and had overlooked the fact that the Association

> . . . appealed to the two most important classes in the country—the priests and the men on the land. . . . [The priests] presided over parish branches of the Association and supervised the collection of "Catholic rent" [dues for the Association] at the church doors after Sunday Mass. The people were roused from their torpor when it was brought home to them that the Association catered to their individual needs.[36]

The Catholic Association enabled the priests to take a far more active political role than would otherwise have been possible, and their status as religious rose even higher among the people because of their involvement in political affairs. The Association did not merely draw upon the assistance of the parish clergy, ". . . it was based upon the parish, with the priests and local worthies as its agents. The messages, speeches, and propaganda of the Catholic Association reached the people from the priests on the altar or in the gatherings outside the Chapel after Mass."[37]

The Association's activities were so effective that a member of the British Parliament, one of the committee investigating the activities of the Association, commented with admiration: "I did not conceive any system of government could be so complete in carrying on communication from heads to inferiors; I thought it a most complete organization for that purpose."[38]

Lacking only its own slate of candidates for political office, the Association was actually a popular, dues-paying political party—the first of its kind in modern times. Its great public following as well as its dependence upon and concern for its local "constituents" suggest that its influence on the Irish who developed the structure and functions of the Democratic parties in American urban areas was more real than imputed.

As an agent of political socialization, the Association acquainted the Irish with a mass-based, a truly popular political organization. It was wholly dependent upon the support of the people and acquainted them with the rudiments of maintaining a political organization composed of small communities. In joining the priests and people within the parish where politics was preached from the pulpit, the Association created the primary Irish political unit, in which essentially everyone shared the same religious and political views.

In 1829 O'Connell agreed to disband the Catholic Association in return for England's granting the Irish the right to sit in Westminster and to hold municipal offices, an action that was formalized by the Catholic Emancipation Act (1829). Nevertheless, the Protestant landowners were successful in barring the Irish from membership in the Irish Parliament, from the office of sheriff in the counties, and prevented their entry to municipal offices until the 1840's. Even then, however, the Irish improved their position only negligibly, and their economic plight went unchanged.

Upon the disbanding of the Association and the passing of the Catholic Emancipation Act, new violence broke out. These uprisings were in part attributable to a new Protestant movement (the New Reformation), originating in northern Ireland, whose purpose was to convert the Catholic Irish. Paralleling this development were new tithe exactions prompted by the religious issue and which led to the Tithe War in the 1830's.

> It had latterly been the custom of the tithe-owners not to demand tithe of the Roman Catholic priests. But a few ardent spirits among the Protestant clergy determined to abandon this politic custom, and the Catholics were more than ever incensed against the exaction of tithes when they found not only that their priests were attacked, but that the money collected was being used for the purpose of proselytism. From this source arose the earlier struggles in the tithe war. The collection of tithe was enforced by large bodies of constabulary and military.[39]

Without the Catholic Association to impose its authority or the English government to implement previously enacted relief legislation, the Irish turned to their usual methods of reprisal. Armed encounters broke out, and the destruction of property and killings were evidence of the widespread activities of the secret societies. The Royal Irish

Constabulary (whose ranks now contained many Catholics) soon quelled the terrorists, and England countered Irish hopes for an end to exploitation with still more temporizing legislation.

By this time the Irish were a thoroughly politicized people, having resorted to secret and open, local and national organizations in their unending efforts to ease their oppression. They had known approximately two centuries of close personal experience with Anglo-Saxon Protestant government, having witnessed how an alien landlord class through its control of government made a mockery of law and a chimera of justice. The Irish disdain of law was probably as important to their future in American city politics as was their knowledge of the ways in which the institutions of Anglo-Saxon government functioned.

The Irish Political Ethos

The most conspicuous aspect of Irish life was that it was set in a context shorn of nearly every influence but raw power. In the ecclesiastical realm, the Irish dwelt under the incontestable power of the Church; in the secular world, they were everywhere subjugated by the power of the landlords and Anglo-Saxon government authorities. It was inevitable, therefore, that the political ethos of the Irish became predominantly power oriented. The conditions of their existence were unaffected by moral influences as a result of the nature of their conflict with England.

The conflict between Ireland and England centered on irreconcilable religious differences. Consequently, it was impossible to develop a common political morality and a political order that could accommodate their conflicting interests. Because the English used their monopoly of government exclusively to further their own ends at the expense of the Irish, the result was to strip the law of all dignity by using it to deprive the Irish of their land, to persecute them for their religious convictions, to exclude them from power, and thereby to transform them into an implacably hostile people.

Since this system rested on a foundation of Anglo-Saxon Protestantism, the power interests of England, and the avarice of the landed aristocracy, the Irish could not obtain justice or acquire respect for the law while they remained Catholic, sought political independence, and desired to have their land restored. Under such conditions moral arguments that sought to remedy Ireland's distress were scarcely more than a clawing at the wind, for the political order that England had established rested on a base of power that went on essentially impervious to moral influences. Such was the history of the Irish with Anglo-Saxon Protestant government.

The Nature of Irish Identity

Irish identity was formed in reaction to the unending economic deprivation and religious persecution suffered under the authoritarian rule of Anglo-Saxon Protestant government and landowners. These inseparable afflictions were the forces that created such remarkable religious solidarity among the Irish and enabled the clergy and hierarchy to assume authoritative roles in their lives. These factors were also the fundamental elements of Irish culture and identity and overlay the norms and customs of families, villages, and towns. As DeBeaumont has so eloquently written:

> Having been forced to struggle for his religion against the Englishman, and for his country against the Protestant, [the Irishman] is accustomed to see partisans of his faith only amongst the defenders of his independence, and to

find devotion to independence only amongst the friends of his religion.

In the midst of the agitations of which his country and his soul have been the theatre, the Irishman who has seen so much ruin consummated within him and around him, believes that there is nothing permanent or certain in the world but his religion—that religion which is coeval with old Ireland—a religion superior to man, ages, and revolutions . . .

In defending his religion, the Irishman has been a hundred times invaded, conquered, driven from his native soil; he kept his faith, and lost his country. But, after the confusion made between these two things in his mind, his rescued religion became his all, and its influence on his heart was further extended by its taking there the place of independence. The altar at which he prayed was his country.

.   .   .   .

The Irish people exists in its church; there alone it is free; there alone it is sure of its rights; there it occupies the only ground that has never given way beneath its feet.[40]

In reaction to the French Revolution's challenge to the authority and interests of the Catholic Church, the Irish prelates so strengthened their position among the Irish that they were henceforth able to make pronouncements with full assurance that their views would neither activate opposition nor stir up criticism. However, their influence was most effective when confined to religious and ideological questions. Their authority had already lost its influence when economic grievances were the cause of popular agitation, and their conservative position on the issues of Irish political representation and independence went unheeded by the people and the activists among them. At the grass roots level, the parish priests were far more influential.

In proclaiming against the French Revolution, the Irish hierarchy identified political liberalism with anti-clericalism and silenced the Irish Catholic liberals, then and for years later, who argued for an egalitarian political regime. In taking this position the hierarchy eliminated the principles of political liberalism as popular symbols for a political morality countervailing the authoritarian government under which Ireland struggled for its existence. As a result, even though the Irish were stirred by a political movement espousing "liberty, equality, and fraternity," they were unable to utilize these secular ideals to give direction to their efforts or breadth and depth of perspective to their outlook.

The subjugation of Ireland had yet another deleterious effect—it became and remained a wholly undeveloped, monistic culture. By controlling the profitable enterprises and by keeping the masses economically and educationally in want, England restricted to a very few those who were able to become intellectually and politically responsive to Ireland's needs. As a result, the Irish did not experience the social and economic ferment and growth that is prerequisite to the development of a society's social organization—that complex of diverse and often competing groups and institutions from which leadership emerges and which generates the variety of interests that provide the impetus for social change and progress.

Then, too, England had established a landed aristocracy in its own image, which it kept dependent in return for the guarantee of wealth and position. Completely subservient to the Crown, this Protestant elite could not have viewed Irish ideologues with a bemused tolerance, as had the French aristocracy with its political writers, because of the religious issue and England's refusal to permit political aberrants to flourish.

As for the Irish, the comparatively few who achieved some success in business, the professions, and agriculture remained politically passive, unable or unwilling to lend their energies and voices to those who hoped to create more widespread support for Irish independence. Few, if any, were so impetuous as to ignore the hazards for affluent Catholics participating in political movements designed to disturb the status quo. Nor did they intercede on behalf of the gallant insurrectionists and publicists whose speeches from the docks eloquently stating the case for Irish self-determination went unheeded. Ireland had no Irish patrons.

By the time of the Great Famine, when hordes of Irishmen emigrated to the United States, Ireland had known English political oppression for approximately two centuries. As the helpless victims of a government whose policies and actions were completely shorn of even moral pretense, the Irish acquired an immutable contempt for and distrust of the law, as well as for those who made, administered, enforced, and interpreted it. The sum of their political experiences forced them to adopt the view that political power was to be sought by all conceivable means, and that it was to be used only in the interests of those who possessed it. This was the dominant political component of their ethnic identity. How important it figured in the lives of the Irish who came to America is seen in Chapters 5 and 6.

The Famine Emigration
and the Early American
Experience

Irish Catholics had been emigrating to the United States
since the end of the eighteenth century. They first came
in sizable numbers after the Revolution in 1798 was put
down by the British, and a steady influx reached American
ports during the next several decades—about 700,000 Irishmen came to this country between 1820 and 1840. But the
truly massive emigration occurred between 1847 and 1851,
when Ireland was engulfed by the Great Famine, which
resulted in the death of thousands from starvation and the
emigration of approximately one million out of a total
population of just over eight million. Emigration continued
over the next half-century as destitution and political unrest sent new waves of Irish peasants to America.

The importance of the Famine Emigration was that it
very suddenly deluged the urban areas of the American

East with great numbers of indigent Irish Catholics. This unexpected inundation of Catholic immigrants had been preceded by over two decades of tension and occasional outbursts of violence stirred up by nativist religious rancor. Now the Irish seemed to be everywhere, and their values and style of life, so starkly obvious in their teeming slum sections of the cities, collided with those of Protestant Americans. The impact of this clash of cultures and social identities was to have an extraordinary bearing on the acculturation and economic opportunities of the Irish—and, in part, also to account for the entry of the Irish into urban politics and for the political style they developed and that continues to be characteristic of many in local politics.

THE FAMINE AND THE EMIGRATION

Ireland's population had risen sharply during the six decades prior to the Great Famine. Land, which had been very scarce, had become almost unobtainable—even tiny plots of marginally productive land were no longer to be found. With less land to support a growing population, many Irish peasants were forced to a hand-to-mouth existence. It became a common sight to see them begging in the country lanes and city streets, for they were unable to support themselves adequately on their bits of land, and employment was so infrequent and so poorly paid that it was of little consequence. After planting their potato crop, many sought laboring jobs in England till harvest required their return.

The number of land holdings was further reduced following the repeal of the Corn Laws (1846), which prompted landlords to turn into pasture much land that had been used to produce grain, thus forcing numbers of Irish peasants off their land into utter destitution.

Because so many Irish had so little land upon which they were entirely dependent for food, there was an imperative need for a crop whose seed was cheap and simple to plant, whose harvest was easy and would feed them for months afterwards, and which was minimally nutritious. The potato met all these requirements and, supplemented with buttermilk, became the dominant crop and staple diet of Ireland. However, the Irish faced a great danger by being so utterly reliant on the potato.

It did not keep, nor could it be stored from one season to another. Thus, every year the nearly two and a half million laborers who had no regular employment more or less starved in the summer, when the old potatoes were finished and the new had not come in. It was for this reason that June, July, and August were called the "meal months"; there was always the danger that potatoes would run out and meal would have to be eaten instead. The laborers would then have to buy it on credit, at exorbitant prices, from the petty dealer and usurer who was the scourge of the Irish village—the dreaded "gombeen-man."[1]

Since the potato was subject to spoilage and because almost none had land enough to harvest a year's supply of food, Irish peasants were often compelled to go into debt to live at the barest level of subsistence. The critical problem was that there was no substitute for the potato in the event of a harvest failure or a blight, and most Irish were unable to buy other food for any length of time if such disaster befell them. When the potato blight struck with its full impact (1845-1848), tragedy became very nearly absolute.

Both England and the United States sent aid to the stricken Irish population, though not enough to provide more than scattered and momentary relief. England's assistance ended as a result of its commitment to laissez-faire economics, which governed its dealing with the root of the problem. That is, government was not to interfere with private enterprise by supplying food to the Irish, for in doing so it would destroy local incentive to remedy the situation. Nor was it to regulate prices so that food might be purchased at reasonable costs, for this would interfere with entrepreneurial freedom. Shipments of food and grain sent by England at the outbreak of the famine were discontinued to conform practice with theory, with the result that hunger and starvation swept over Ireland.

These horrible conditions were rendered even more severe by the landlords' practice of evicting Irish peasants who had no way of meeting their rent payments. "Ireland was a conquered country, the Irish peasant a dispossessed man, his landlord an alien conqueror. There was no paternalism such as existed in England, no hereditary loyalty or feudal tie."[2] Quite literally, the Irish had no one to whom they could turn for help. The conclusion they drew from the disaster of the famine, and which is generally held by them today, is that it was caused by yet another act of English oppression—for in the midst of deaths on every side and the hordes of those seeking escape from starvation by emigrating, grain and cattle continued to be exported to England from the farms of the landowners.

The following description of the famine is one of the many accounts of the suffering found in most parts of rural Ireland. It is inserted here to emphasize the grim memory carried by the emigrants to this country, part of the bitter legacy they passed on to subsequent generations.

> The people died on the roads, and they died in the fields; they died on the mountains, and they died in the glens; they died at the relief works and they died in their houses, so that little streets and villages were left almost without an inhabitant; and at last some few, despairing of help in the country, crawled into the town, and died at the doors of residents and outside the union walls. . . . All this took place because there was no one there with sufficient ad-

ministrative capacity to import corn in time, and to bring the food and people together.[3]

The English people were genuinely concerned about the plight of the Irish, but even had this been generally known among the Irish it would doubtless have been a matter of unimportance. English concern and sympathy would probably have been suspect, for the more extreme Irish Protestant newspapers promptly introduced the religious issue by calling the emigration ".... a flight from the 'tyranny of priests' and the 'endless exactions' of the Catholic Church. So long as the Irish remained under the 'poisonous influence' of the Church, they would remain 'inert and useless' and their only recourse was to escape by emigrating."[4]

The extremist Catholic newspapers also stressed the role of the religious conflict, arguing that the famine ".... was a deliberate scheme on the part of Britain to depopulate the country"[5] in order to bring about the complete submission of the Irish. Thus did the religious animus infect the famine-stricken land as the Irish fled to America, hopeful for a chance to begin a new life.

Since the concern here is with the conditions the Irish found in America rather than with the terrible hardships they endured on the ships that brought them here, suffice it to say that most embarked on the voyage with barely enough funds to pay for passage and food, and were often victimized at the ports at both ends of the journey by avaricious middle-men who cheated them with exorbitant or fictitious charges for food, transportation, and lodging. The Irish reached America as a thoroughly downtrodden people, with searing memories of religious persecution and devastating economic hardship.

It would have been exceptional for a people so thoroughly alien to their new land to enjoy the same degree of social and economic mobility as resident Americans. In fact this did not generally occur for the Irish until well into the twentieth century, and until then the Irish maintained the identity they had acquired in Ireland. The causes for their social and economic exclusion will be discussed in this and the next chapter.

THE EARLY AMERICAN EXPERIENCE:
THE URBAN SETTLERS

The Irish became urban dwellers out of necessity although they were really a rural people. Yet few, if any, had really farmed—they were generally cotters or squatters who had never truly belonged to an agricultural class. Subsisting on the produce from small plots that required little skill in planting or harvesting, they had been essentially field laborers and, as such, were completely without experience in transforming expanses of fertile land into fields of grain. Nor had they ever had the opportunity to own, raise, or care for herds of cattle. Consequently, they had little thought of beginning anew in the farmlands of the Midwest, the journey to which was too costly had it appealed to them.

It was logical for the Irish to settle in the eastern cities since they were generally illiterate and unskilled, and reached American ports with just enough money for a few days' lodging and sparse fare. The urban centers provided them with far more opportunities for work than did most small towns, where industry and commerce were not so thriving or expansive. Moreover, the urban areas offered them the welcome sight of those who had preceded them and of the parishes that at once gave them a comforting sense of community in their new setting. The parish church was there to minister to their spiritual needs, to draw them under its protective mantle against the hostile Protestant society about them. Although a few priests spoke out against the grisly conditions of slum life that imprisoned more and more of the Irish, urging them to move to the Midwest and to turn to farming and a happier and healthier life in the open spaces, these were adamantly opposed by prominent spokesmen of the Church. The latter feared that those who heeded such advice would be lost to the faith where there were no priests to conduct Mass, to hear confession, and to build a church and exercise tutelage over the parish community.

The vast numbers of those who left Ireland moved into the cities, where they formed great concentrations of indigent "foreigners" who immediately encountered considerable resentment because they were Catholic and of the lower class. The Irish soon comprised the first huge pool of manual workers, the first truly proletarian labor force of this nation's urban areas which were gradually becoming hubs of industry and commerce.

Irish Solidarity: The Influence of Class, Religion, and Irish Nationalism

Eager to accept almost any employment they could find, the Irish soon moved into the occupations available to the unskilled—stevedores, teamsters, common laborers. Many found work with construction gangs, helping to raze or erect buildings and becoming the bulwark of the itinerant work forces that built the roads, canals, and railroads connecting the East with the Midwest and beyond. Then, as now, work was periodic or seasonal for unskilled laborers, and competition for jobs was a constant threat. The oversupply of labor was at least one factor that intensified the beginning problems in race relations. The Irish, literally fighting each other for the scarce supply of jobs, came to regard the Negro not as one more oppressed than themselves or as a fellow-sufferer, but as a menace to their own very precarious existence.

The economic lot of the Irish in the cities was extraordinarily depressing. The little they earned was often drained by helping to purchase passage to America for those of their families who remained in Ireland. And, social barriers aside, their meager incomes forced them to live in squalid slums and tenements which, with taverns at every turn, were constant inducement to seek escape or commiseration in drink. Many Irishmen succumbed to excessive drinking which, despite whatever temporary release it may have afforded them from the duress of life, effectively helped blot out realistic hopes and possibilities for the better life they wanted so desperately for themselves and their children.[6]

By the end of the Civil War the Irish were prisoners of the vicious circle that was to hold them social captives until well into the twentieth century. Spurned as lower-class menials and discriminated against as Catholics, they were caught in economic and social conditions that prevented them from improving their material circumstances and changing their social style.

The social style and values of the Irish were viewed by Protestant Americans in terms of the religious cleavage that identified the Irish as "Catholics"—people who were hopelessly quarrelsome, verging on social dereliction, and both incapable and undesirous of self-improvement. Catholicism was the most convenient symbol with which to stereotype the Irish, and through it the Irish represented the least desirable social and religious element. What is more, Catholicism was also looked upon as the one religious doctrine that constituted a direct threat to democratic government. Well before the Civil War the religious conflict between Protestants and Catholics had become the pivotal issue that was to dominate all others directly affecting the Irish for many decades to come.

Anti-Catholic sentiment had so pervaded America even in Colonial times that religious epithets were customarily used by "native" Americans to describe the social traits of the few Catholics then living among them. Religious prejudice was so widespread that Catholics enjoyed full civil rights and freedom of religion only in Rhode Island. In 1690, when the English went to war with France and Spain, all Catholics (and there were very few) in the British colonies were regarded as potential enemies. It was taken for granted that their religious allegiance to Rome would necessarily supersede their loyalty to England. And it was feared, if unrealistically, that they would actively and enthusiastically aid the French in Canada and the Spanish in Florida.

Shortly after the turn of the eighteenth century Maryland enacted legislation that levied a substantial tax on Irish servants in order to prevent "the importing of too great a number of Irish papists." During this time the eastern colonies enacted statutes very similar to the Penal Laws that England imposed on Ireland during the same period; Catholics in the colonies were forbidden to own arms, to serve in the militia, and were compelled to pay taxes in addition to those everyone paid.

This mood of religious discrimination persisted through the Revolutionary period, abating somewhat after the alliance with France in 1778, but it was too firmly imbedded to dissipate. The principles contained in the Declaration of Independence not only did not signify the abatement of this religious prejudice, the First Amendment's separation of church and state was clearly inspired by it.

The first years of the republic contrasted the formality of the legal equality accorded Catholics with the practice of inequality; Catholics were still considered potentially dangerous. The Federalist party became the political force that kept alive the nativists' suspicion and fear of "Papists and foreigners." It was the Federalists who authored the Alien Act of 1798, which extended the period of naturalization from five to fourteen years, a measure whose real object was to restrict Irish immigration. The Alien and Sedition Acts, enacted the same year at the instigation of the Federalists, were directed at the Irish Catholic immigrants fleeing the aftermath of the Revolution of 1798 and who tried to foment insurrection in Ireland from the United States.

As the years passed and Irish communities began to burgeon, the popular mood grew more resentful of Catholics. The Irish bore the brunt of mob violence when, in 1831, religious tensions exploded and nativists burned a convent in Charlestown, Massachusetts. During this same decade Maria Monk's, *Awful Disclosures,* a fabricated, despicable tale of lurid behavior in a convent found a wide enough audience to sell 300,000 copies between the time of its first printing and the Civil War. In 1844, street rioting broke out in Philadelphia when Protestants, objecting to the school board's decision to permit Catholic children to read the Douay version of the bible in public schools, stormed through the Irish sections of the city.

The flood of Irish into urban America in the late 1840's greatly intensified the religious issue, which had now spread well beyond the cities in which they settled. Swarming into the eastern cities, the Irish alarmed the native Americans who feared for the very survival of their social and political order. The invasion of illiterate Catholic immigrants convinced them that their way of life was at stake. Earlier, nativist anxiousness about and resentment of the influx of Catholics was expressed in discriminatory statutes and later, in periodic isolated incidents of violence and through anti-Catholic literature. With the Famine Emigration, however, the multitude of Irish Catholics pouring into the cities was visualized by nativists as a fearful menace to be contained, if not eliminated, by concerted, widespread political action. Thus was the Know-Nothing movement born in 1854.

In the view of the nativists, Catholicism was an alien belief allied to several foreign cultures, but it became most identified with the Irish, who were its arch exponents and defenders and who were to fight the battle of religious discrimination for all other Catholic immigrants who came to America in their wake. The religious issue contained within it another of broader significance—that of admittance to full membership in society itself. It was exceedingly difficult for Irish Catholic immigrants both to feel and become accepted by their new land since Protestantism and Americanism had long been synonymous. Commenting on the significance of this fusion of religion and nationality, Herberg has remarked:

> Normally, to be born an American meant to be a Protestant; this was the religious identification that in the American mind quite naturally went along with being an American. Non-Protestants felt the force of this conviction almost as strongly as did the Protestants; Catholics and Jews, despite their vastly increasing numbers, experienced their non-Protestant religion as a problem, even as an obstacle, to their becoming full-fledged Americans: it was a mark of their foreignness.[7]

An external influence reinforcing Irish identity in the United States was Ireland's continuing economic plight and recurring efforts to win independence from England. Letters from home or tales from newly arrived immigrants rekindled the memories of their own suffering in Ireland or inflamed their feelings with fresh accounts of misfortunes borne by friends and relatives. Feeling very much bound together by "the strong tie of bearing one common wrong," the Irish in the United States started a variety of movements to liberate Ireland, all of which were disastrous failures. Each one activated competing factions, some were led by opportunists interested in acclaim and money, and none was successful in drawing popular support from the Irish.

One of these groups, the Fenians, achieved a degree of notoriety by actually undertaking an invasion of Canada after the Civil War in the hope of winning Federal support on the basis of England's assistance to the South during the Civil War. Such a venture, it was hoped, would result in a declaration of war by the United States which, following its victory about which the Fenians were certain, would promptly force England to grant Ireland its independence. The invading Irish, with high hopes and few forces, were immediately repulsed or captured by the Canadian troops. The United States government intervened only to obtain the release of the captured Fenian leaders and to thwart their hopes for another attack. Despite the utter ineffectiveness of the Fenians and other "liberation" organizations, the clamor they raised in behalf of Irish self-determination did much to keep this issue alive among the Irish in America.

The issue of Ireland's independence made itself felt in American politics. In the presidential campaigns after the Civil War some of the candidates thought it expedient to express sympathy for Ireland's cause in their search for Irish votes. England's refusal to head Ireland's nearly three centuries-old agitation for freedom was responsible for the Irish allegation that World War I was ". . . Britain's war—a war to maintain and strengthen British world domination. [The Irish] were almost wholly against it. Why, the Irish-American asked, are the English so anxious to liberate Belgium when they themselves hold Ireland in subjection?"[8] And "when Mayor Curley of Boston spoke out on behalf of Great Britain, the *Gaelic American* denounced him as a 'yellow dog' prepared to sell out to the Anglo-Saxons."[9] Big Bill Thompson, when campaigning for election as Chicago's mayor in 1919, catered to the Irish (and German) vote by publicly threatening to "punch the King of England on the nose" if he set foot in Chicago.

Until Ireland won its independence in 1922, Irish nationalism exerted a powerful influence on the Irish in America; it constantly reminded them that Erin still bore the weight of Anglo-Saxon Protestant tyranny and that their own plight in the United States was also due to Anglo-Saxon Protestant discrimination. Irish nationalism did not subside even after Ireland became free, because England kept its control over Ulster (Northern Ireland), where Protestants were in the majority and where Ireland's commercial wealth was located. This issue began to lose its strength as an ethnocentric force only as the new generations of American Irish were removed ever further from the old memories and as they moved ever more fully into the assimilation process.

IRISH IDENTITY IN AMERICA: THE ALIENATED

Then, as now, assimilation was equated with conformity to middle-class, Protestant values of work, education, leisure, and propriety, and this association of middle-class standards with Protestantism confronted the Irish as an insurmountable social barrier. Their social habits reflected their coarseness, scant education, the habits of slum living, the conditions under which they worked, and the menial jobs in which they labored. Religious differences aside, everything about their existence militated against their emulating the social standards set for them by Protestant-American society. But since the profound social and cul-

tural differences between these two groups were anchored
in the religious cleavage, the social "shortcomings" of the
Irish were inevitably attributed to their religion.

Understandably, the Irish reacted in kind, rejecting and
vilifying as "Protestant" the values and style of life of the
dominant society. Smarting because they were ostracized
by native American society and rankled by the unending
criticism that accused them of critically threatening the
values and character of the American social order, the Irish
were defended through ecclesiastic voices, their only
spokesmen. The *Boston Reporter,* the medium of the Diocese, replied to nativist critics that labor was both honor-
able and indispensable to the progress of the nation, at-
tributing to it a dignity and respectability that the Irish
would attach to it for years to come. Obliged to distinguish
between Irish and Americans, it editorialized:

> Will Americans go into quarries and hew out solid rocks?
> Will they go into morasses and dykes and creeks of the
> forest, and hew out and establish a railroad or a continuous
> canal? . . . Will the Americans . . . labor in the wasting
> drudgery of metal foundries, glass furnaces, and other
> similar occupations, which require the bone and sinew,
> and robust constitutions, which *Irishmen alone* can bring
> into such labors? No! they will not do this work. If it de-
> pended upon them, it would remain undone.[10]

Physical labor, if strenuous, dirty, and dangerous, became a mark of honor among the Irish, who for years to
come took pride in their physical robustness and in jobs
requiring a *man's* strength. As late as the 1920's, James
Tully, author of *Shanty Irish,* was able to write unself-
consciously of his grandfather's open pride in his later years
of his superior ability to swing a pick and use a shovel while
digging ditches for the government on Ohio roads.

The regard the Irish gave to laboring jobs, however, em-
phasized their social distance from the Protestant urban

middle class which set the standards of social respectability, and added to the already great difficulties the Irish
faced in improving their social and economic status.

Out of such work was born a toughness of body and
temperament that was reinforced by the social pressures
confronting the Irish. Enduring economic hardship,
scorned as "papists" and "idolators," the friendless Irish
clung ever more tenaciously to their religion, whose spiritual sustenance eased their burdens. Like the Irish, Christ
had suffered persecution, privation, and scorn, and in their
eyes He seemed to be a martyr for them alone. The following poignant reflection describes the solace of religion upon
which so many of these hapless people depended.

> When we luck at him there, we see our blessed Saviour,
> stripped a'most naked lake ourselves; whin we luck at the
> crown i'thorns on the head, we see the Jews mockin' him,
> jist the same as—some people mock ourselves for our re-
> ligion; whin we luck at his eyes, we see they wor never dry,
> like our own; whin we luck at the wound in his side, why
> we think less of our own wounds an' bruises we got 'ithin
> and 'ithout, every day av our lives.[11]

The historical religious and class cleavages between the
Irish Catholics and Anglo-Saxon Protestants had found in
America a new climate in which to flourish. The Irish,
abused and alienated by native Americans, took refuge in
and dignified what made them distinctive from Protestant-
American society—their religion, occupations, social perspective, and style of life. Unlike some of the other European immigrants who came to America a generation or
more after them, the Irish did not deliberately search out
the more practical paths leading to assimilation. They had
almost no choice. On the other hand, most Irish refused
to acknowledge any superiority in the established social
standards, deriding the ethos and norms of the middle class
in their bitterness over the effective segregation imposed

upon them and the religious discrimination everywhere besetting them.

The distinctive symbols of Irish identity retained their vitality in the United States through the nineteenth and well into the twentieth century. Their strength sprang from and was renewed by the bitterness over the religious and class differences that were nearly as acute and divisive as they had been in Ireland between Protestant landowners and Irish peasants. They also fed upon the cause of Irish nationalism, which focused on and highlighted these differences.

Nevertheless, retention of their identity posed a problem for the Irish. As immigrants who were anxious to enjoy the wonderful opportunities said to await everyone who came to America with a desire to work, they quickly found that access to a bountiful, happy existence was dependent upon possessing the social credentials honored by Protestant-American society. The Irish were quickly informed how unwelcome they were as lower-class, Catholic aliens.

Denied membership in the established society, they reacted by cutting themselves off from meaningful contact with the American middle class and remained largely isolated from and resistant to much of the major social change occurring in the nation through the first half of the twentieth century. The cultural conflict that precipitated this separatist drift was undeniably fundamental. Still, the particularities of its impact were the result of certain Catholic institutional influences.

Symbols of Irish Identity and Alienation   *4*

It is not enough to say that the Irish found themselves social outcasts in America, for the vicissitudes of life might have eroded their dominant cultural values and, therefore, their social identity and thus dispersed them faster and drawn them more quickly into the assimilation process.

As it was, there were powerful internal and external forces reinforcing their ethnic identity and solidarity, constraints that both gave them an overriding sense of social distinctiveness and kept them isolated from the society within which they became an enclave. These constraints were: the conservatism of the Irish clergy who rose to power in the Catholic Church; the exclusive character of the parochial school system and the nature of its educational emphasis; and the nature of the initial experiences of the Irish with the ideology, ends, and advocates of the Reform Movement in the generation before the Civil War.

Each of these constraints effectively impeded the assim-

ilation of the Irish. The second and third were also especially instrumental in helping to create and maintain cohesive Irish communities whose physical and cultural
symbol was the parish church.

Before discussing the development and effects of these
ethnocentric influences, it is pertinent to examine the nature of the assimilation process* in order to determine why
these constraints had such inhibiting effects on the assimilation of the Irish.

As Gordon has pointed out, assimilation is a complex
process with two very different aspects which he terms
"behavioral" and "structural."[1] The former connotes adop-
tion of the "cultural behavior pattern of the 'host' society,"[2]
involves essentially impersonal relationships with the larger
society with which the newcomers have begun to identify,
and is thus a process of identification with national symbols rather than of social interaction. Because these symbols are national, it is possible for an immigrant to say, "I
am an American," proudly salute the flag and honor national holidays, and be unquestionably patriotic in both
attitude and action. Despite such commitment, he may
have no really meaningful social contact with other groups
in society and be regarded as socially unacceptable by the
dominant (and even less influential) strata in society.
"Behavioral" assimilation alone has only a slightly modify-
ing effect on ethnic characteristics, values, and behavior,
for the ethnic group is socially unrelated to the dominant
groups and mores of society which are the transforming
agents in the acculturation process.

"Structural" assimilation, on the other hand, refers to
the social engagement of the immigrant group with the
"cliques, organizations, institutional activities, and general civic life of the receiving society."[3] This phase of the

---

* This section draws on Milton M. Gordon, "Assimilation in
America," *Daedalus*, Spring, 1961.

assimilation process is specifically concerned with endur-ing personal social relationships. Because it signifies work-ing and socializing with individuals from other groups, it is contingent upon the existence of opportunities for the re-laxation, weakening, and ultimate disintegration of the elemental components of ethnic identity. The attenuation of this identity is most often accomplished as a result of continuing involvement in the work, educational, and lei-sure processes of society through which individuals become "structurally" related to each other.

These processes are the catalysts responsible for the at-trition of ethnic solidarity, which gradually disintegrates as the ethnic group adopts the symbols and values of the dominant society—and has thus begun to assimilate. The process of assimilation, therefore, "normally" requires three generations to produce the acculturated American; the first generation American, who is caught between the values and life style of his immigrant parents and the American "way of life" that is idealized in the public schools and communication media, represents to his children a com-posite of "old country" and American values and customs. This indecisive admixture is given a nearly completing assimilating thrust by the exposure of his children to the amalgamation of distinctly American social, economic, and political values, processes, and events they encounter at school and at play.

It is because the Irish, as was true of all other European immigrants, were first drawn into the "behavioral" assimi-lation process that there was no paradox in their enthusi-astic, and at times militant, patriotism even though simul-taneously they were socially disfranchised. "Behavioral" assimilation is the process by which all citizens are first as-sociated with the nation and its government and through which they support it. This is all the more true in times of external threats to national security, for when national sur-

vival is the transcendental issue and the enemy is impersonal, the emotionality with which such a crisis is imbued
subordinates questions of social justice until the danger has
passed. The cause is national and is not susceptible of significantly varying interpretations by the various minority
groups if they eagerly want, as they usually do, full membership in society.

For these reasons it is understandable that the exploits
and traditions of the "Fighting Sixty-Ninth" (the Irish
Regiment from New York City) date from the Civil War,
when appallingly large numbers of Irishmen died in Union
colors. Despite a draft riot by the Irish in New York City
that was caused by what they believed to be a discriminatory conscription statute, the Irish served the cause of the
Union with valor and daring, frequently volunteering for
the first waves of attack in which so many of them died. As
alienated from society as their parishioners, the Irish clergy,
the authoritative spokesmen for the Irish, were also zealous
in their support of a Union victory. Their attitude toward
the Civil War

> . . . was that expressed by Rev. John McMullen, President
> of the University of St. Mary's of the Lake, in Chicago,
> who said, "If it were not that I am a priest and a man of
> peace, I would be down South with my old companions
> who are still alive, fighting under the Stars and Stripes
> for the preservation of the Union."[4]

Yet even the generally recognized commitment of the
Irish to the cause of the Union did not change. the esteem
in which they were held nor encourage them to appear
more "acceptable," to "qualify" for membership in the
"host" society. It might have been expected that the social
dynamics of war would have improved somewhat the status
of the Irish, but certain events had occurred prior to the
Civil War, the origin of some of them predating the

Famine immigration, which were responsible for the Irish remaining outside the pale of "structural" assimilation for decades to come. One of inestimable importance was the rise of the Irish clergy to power in the Catholic Church in the United States.

Irish Prelates and the American Catholic Church

The Irish won control of the hierarchy of the American Catholic Church because they were politically skillful and because so many of them were strategically located. As the originally dominant French clergy began to lose influence through lack of replacements, their position was also weakened by the influx of priests from Ireland to the American urban areas where parishes and communicants proliferated. This vast increase of churches and parishioners in the urban centers facilitated the Irish priests' capturing influential positions in the Church, for diocesan authority is most often centered in a large urban area from which it supervises its network of parishes. In contrast to the Germans, who settled in the midwestern farmlands as well as in the cities, the great concentration of Irish immigrants was in the expanding cities and provided a substantial base for, as well as a claim and access to, power. By the time the Poles, Italians, Czechs, and other Catholics emigrated to the United States, the Irish had won a commanding position in the Church, which they would hold for years to come.

The concern to provide sufficient numbers of priests for the Irish who came to America originated in Ireland, where the Church for decades had been troubled about maintaining the faith of those who had left Ireland. Ireland's prelates fully realized that these urban immigrants would be exposed to religious laxity, indifference, and efforts to proselytize them unless there were enough priests and churches to minister to their needs and bolster their commitment to the faith. At least periodic attendance at Mass and confession was necessary if the Church was not to risk losing its communicants.

Deeply aware of the necessity to secure and staff the Church in America, the hierarchy in Ireland took action even before the Great Famine.

> As early as 1842 a seminary was established in Dublin for the specific purpose of training Irish priests as missionaries for American and other English speaking countries in which Irish emigrants settled. The seminary, All Hallows, tried as best it could to meet the increasing demand for Irish priests and in the century following its founding sent out more than a thousand to the United States.[5]

This steady, sizable flow of Irish priests into the urban parishes increased their numbers at all levels in the Church and assisted them in capturing the most powerful positions in the American Catholic hierarchy. Once they had established their control of the Church it was very easy, especially in view of their numerical superiority, to bring other Irish priests to positions of influence. The continuing dominance of the Irish in the Church for decades after the Famine immigration prompted Thomas Sugrue to write of them:

> This was the Church into which I was baptized in 1907. The Irish clergy ran it; they dominated its organization, its hierarchy, and its point of view; they set the pattern which oriented newcomers first to Americanism, then to American Catholicism. They were disliked and resented—quietly— by priests of other immigrant groups, who came from countries in which the aristocracy and the intelligentsia traditionally stood guard over the natural inclination of the clergy to exploit its relationship with the peasant classes, and who therefore were accustomed to performing their religious duties and to leaving well enough alone.[6]

It is true, as Monsignor John Tracy Ellis has suggested, that the Church's energies and attention were almost entirely absorbed by the laborious task of building churches and establishing "a school system such as no other Catholic national community had ever attempted."[7] On the other hand, it is not wholly accurate to suggest that because of this concentration of interest and resources that ". . . Catholic leaders, both clerical and lay, manifested relatively little concern for the broad moral and ethical issues that were . . . engag[ing] the attention of older American groups."[8] The secular policies promulgated by Irish prelates had historically been guided by the political context of the times; in Ireland they had either taken a distinctly conservative position on the dominant issues or deliberately avoided comment when acting otherwise might have jeopardized the Church's security. The most influential of them scarcely modified this position in the United States until after World War II. Before then, individual Irish prelates who were in the vanguard of social reform found themselves acting against the climate of opinion in the Church, as the following attests.

> [Until 1869] the Knights of Labor had been a secret organization, as were all early associations of employees. This led to condemnation by the Roman Catholic Church, which [was traditionally] opposed to secret societies. Not all the officials of the church condemned Powderly and the Knights of Labor, however. Some Catholic bishops, including Bishop Richard Gilmour of Cleveland, spoke up for Powderly and publicly expressed their sympathy with the struggle of the working men for a better living. But at one point Roman Catholic opposition to the Knights of Labor was so strong that Powderly was charged both with being a Mason and a Molly Maguire. It would be hard to think of two societies more radically opposed.[9]

Certain of the Irish hierarchy, such as Cardinal Gibbons and Archbishop Ireland, may very well have influenced both clergy and laity in Baltimore and St. Paul, where they respectively held authority, but they had very little success in liberalizing the views of the Irish conservatives who dominated the American Catholic Church. Discussing the negative attitude of the Catholic hierarchy toward his interest in establishing a journal dedicated to social reform just before World War I, Monsignor John Ryan, a noted Irish liberal, wrote:

> . . . I put the matter before the Cardinal Archbishop, His Eminence John M. Farley. His reply and attitude were unfavorable. This is not surprising, for I was still regarded as "too radical" by many Bishops as well as others; moreover, very few members of the hierarchy at that time [1914] were sufficiently interested in the social question to appreciate the need or the utility of such a publication.[10]

For reasons to be discussed later in this chapter, the Irish hierarchy—and the Irish—had ample cause for refusing to heed the calls to join the movements seeking to achieve substantial improvements in the living and working conditions of the poor. Without the authoritative voice · of the Church encouraging them to support even the basic economic issues with which labor began to grapple after the Civil War, the Irish remained a people of the parish, where the priest was the authority in most affairs immediately affecting their lives.

The Influence of the Priests

The bond that had developed between the priests and the people in Ireland lost none of its strength and effectiveness for many years after the first large waves of Irish immigrants settled in the cities. Until the appearance of local politicians and the more prosperous saloonkeepers, the priests were the only influential figures in the Irish communities, those alone to whom the Irish could turn for advice and assistance. It was the priests who imparted a sense of security to their parishioners struggling to find their way in this inhospitable land, and who were able to comfort them in their hardships by reassuring them of the meaning of the natural order in which they were such harassed *dramatis personae*. The priests retained their close relationship with the people, joining the men who built the canals and railroads, moving with those who left the cities to work in the coal mines, and staying with others who established small Irish communities in the small towns along the newly built railroads.

In the cities the priests went among the people, intimately sharing their few joys and unending troubles. The trust they earned was given substantial financial support that was all the more remarkable in view of the generally indigent circumstances of the Irish. As early as 1868, for example, Chicago had

> . . . about 20 Catholic churches, for a Catholic population of about 60,000 of whom 50,000 were Irish; and other churches . . . were either in the course of erection or in active contemplation. There were 12,000 Catholic children, of all classes and conditions of life, receiving a sound Catholic teaching in academies and parochial schools.[11]

In other cities with sizable Irish communities the number of churches built was equally impressive, and parochial school construction—and enrollments—kept pace. In San Francisco, too, where the Irish had been urged to settle because of the comparative absence of religious bigotry, the Church prospered. In the 1860's its property,

> . . . including buildings and real estate, was valued at 2,010,000 dollars. This included the cathedral and five other churches, convents, asylums, and hospitals. Giving Cath-

olics of other nationalities full credit for their liberality,
and allowing for the generous assistance afforded by those
of different denominations, it is admitted that three-fourths
of what has been done for the church, the city, and county
of San Francisco has been done by the Irish. In fact, without them little could have been done; but with them everything was possible.[12]

This seemingly immodest conclusion appears fully justified in view of the unstinting support the Irish have typically given the Church over the years, a generosity born
out of their intensely personal relationship to Catholicism
and to their priests.

The influential role of the priest, in conjunction with the
force of their uniquely adverse religious experiences in
both Ireland and America, has inclined the Irish, far more
than any other European Roman Catholic group, to recruit for the Church. It has traditionally been the Irish hope
that one son in each family will enter the priesthood (and
one daughter a sisterhood). As Father James Shannon has
observed:

> It has been remarked that the Irish religion is not a bond
> with the Church as an organization and still less with the
> Church as a place, but rather a personal bond between
> the Irish people and their priests. . . . And in the Irish
> homes, in the United States as in Ireland, there was created
> an admirable tradition of respect for the priesthood and
> the religious life. Family prayers frequently asked for the
> grace of a religious vocation in the family. The history
> of the Irish in America demonstrates how effectively these
> prayers have been answered.[13]

Because of the status of the priests and the importance
of the parish church as the one institutional bulwark in a
Protestant society, Irish social organizations became per-
manently associated with the parish church, where they

were under the surveillance of the pastor. These Irish Catholic associations—the various Sodalities, the Holy Name Society, the social, athletic, and community organizations—and their activities were the social sinews of Irish solidarity and separatism. Unlike the various societies that other immigrants formed to pay for the passage of their families to America or to anticipate burial expenses, these groups have endured (or developed) through the years. It is so typical for them to be attached to the parish church that an Irish priest stated during an interview, "my instinctive response, and I'm from a thoroughly American Irish neighborhood, is that I'd be suspicious of unrelated [to the parish] Irish neighborhood organizations. I'd think they were Protestant."

Personifying their most deeply held values, their alienation from society, and serving as the focal point of the Irish communities upon whose support they could fully rely, the Irish pastors held great sway over their parishioners.[14] In reality, they "governed" many of the social activities of the people through their ecclesiastical authority and because of their special relationship to them. Their influence was discussed by the pastor of a largely Irish parish who said:

> The Irish pastor *ran* his parish. The Church was very important as an Irish instrument for community organization and advancement, for protection. They [the pastors] were great builders, built all kinds of schools and churches, always felt they could dictate to the politicians without too much trouble. They could get people on the fire and police [departments].

Where the Irish community lives on today, the Irish pastor exercises much the same influence as did his predecessors. One whose church is in such a community acknowledged this, candidly stating that:

> The people do look on the pastor as a leader. . . . Some would even say I'm king, and if I died they'd say, "the king is dead." They really do revere the priest and seek his advice from top to bottom. Maybe I'm an old one. From a place like this they come looking for jobs. If there's any trouble they come to you. They sometimes feel, "who else have I got to turn to but the leader?"

Contrasting the authority of the older with the younger Irish pastors, and noting the growing importance of lay influence in parish affairs, a young Irish priest observed:

> The Irish pastor tends to be very suspicious of lay activities. Irish pastors—what decisions have to be made, they'll make them. It's not so true any more, because pastors have to get the support of the parishioners. But some like Monsignor _____ still runs his parish as he sees fit.

Under the aegis of their priests, bound together by their special feelings and experiences as communicants of Catholicism, and stigmatized by society as detested proletarian aliens, the Irish were socially situated to be highly resistant to the attractions and currents of change in the urban areas —the magnetic elements of assimilation. As effective as any other factor in retarding their entry into the "structural" assimilation process was their separatist system of education, whose organization, curriculum, and emphases were designed and controlled by the Irish hierarchy and clergy.

THE PAROCHIAL SCHOOL SYSTEM: EDUCATIONAL AND SOCIAL SEPARATISM

The decision to establish a Catholic system of education completely separated from the American public schools actually originated in Ireland in 1849. This action

was prompted by the renewed proselytizing efforts of Protestants in the north of Ireland, and especially by their proposal to create nondenominational schools to teach both
Protestant and Catholic children who would receive common religious instruction. The conservative and more
powerful faction of Ireland's hierarchy, under the leadership of Archbishop McHale, was adamantly opposed to this
nonsectarian educational plan, firmly convinced that it was
no more than an insidious plot whose real object was the
conversion of the young, unsuspecting Catholic children.
A spokesman of the church soon condemned it, declaring

> . . . it to be "contrary to the spirit and practice of our Holy
> Church to sanction united religious instruction, or to sanc-
> tion any instruction in matters connected with religion
> given to Catholics by persons who themselves reject the
> teachings of the Catholic Church." . . . From that time
> denominational education became one of the chief of the
> Catholic claims.[15]

The Irish clergy in the United States were equally committed to a Church-controlled system of education. For the
greater part of the nineteenth century most of them had
come from or received their training in Ireland, where
there was but one view on religious issues. Once associated with American parishes they had grown increasingly
anxious about the "flavor of Protestantism" that had crept
into the public schools through the use of the King James
version of the Bible—they regarded the "Lord's prayer as
being Protestant in form." So dangerous an influence dram-
atized the need for exclusively Catholic schools. With
such schools Catholic students, a minority in the public
schools, could avoid exposure to the deceptive and nefarious
influences of Protestant values. So gravely concerned had
the Irish become about the issue of education that in the
East, where religious animosities were especially virulent,

Irish parents were known to prevent their children from attending public schools when there were no parochial schools available. In Boston, for example, where

> . . . parochial schools were inadequate or non-existent, many of the children attended no school at all. In 1877, some 9,000 of the 43,000 children in Boston between the ages of five and fifteen were not in school, and most of them were Irish. A first generation Irish son, deprived of his education by his parents' beliefs, often remained as ignorant as his immigrant father.[16]

The breach between the Irish Catholic and Protestant religious and educational values was widened by the early efforts of the Catholic Church to obtain public funds to help reduce the heavy financial burden it assumed for its parochial schools.* Archbishop John Hughes of New York spearheaded the effort by urging the state legislature to enact a bill assisting all educational institutions. Such a petition by so prominent a member of the Catholic hierarchy was probably doomed at the outset; at any rate, he was entirely unsuccessful, and his action greatly exacerbated the popular fear and distrust of Catholics.

The parochial school institutionalized the religious and secular differences dividing the Irish from Protestant Americans. Not only was it the most effective means of impressing young Catholic students with the special significance of religious values and attitudes and in isolating them from other students, but it also and inevitably maintained the social distance between the Irish and the outer society. This was so because, regardless of the emphasis on academic achievement that the parochial school system then

---

* This action was begun before the Civil War, before the Fourteenth Amendment had been incorporated in the Constitution, extending to the states the First Amendment's prohibition of the use of government funds in support of undertakings of religious institutions or groups.

placed or came to favor, the system was only secondarily committed to education; it had been created through ecclesiastic edict for the principal purpose of maintaining the faith of Catholic children.

Purely educational matters, therefore, for years remained necessarily subordinate to religious ones. The responsibility for attending to the latter was considered so important that only a few decades after the introduction of parochial schools the American hierarchy, now controlled by the Irish, concluded that the system should no longer be optional. Pastors *must* build parochial schools and all Catholic children *must* attend them.

> . . . the experience of their predecessors made the bishops of the 1880's and 1890's surer of their footing [with regard to the indispensability of parochial schools]. In their minds they were accountable before God for the religious training of both native and immigrant Catholic children. They knew that earlier bishops had tried to reach an understanding with the public school system and had failed. If they would still their conscience, therefore, there was but one recourse left to them, regardless of what other Americans might think of the parochial school. That was to make the parochial school almost mandatory upon their priests and people, and this they did for the first time in the Third Plenary Council of Baltimore in 1884 with the result that by 1900 the number of such schools had been increased to nearly 4,000.[17]

The parochial school was primarily responsible in two ways for keeping alive the special identity of the Irish. First, its ethos was, above all, religious, pervading the lives of the students during all their school years. Second, because Irish Catholics did not become socially diversified for many decades they unquestioningly accepted clerical authority over educational content and retained their separatist educational and social attitudes.

The ethos of the schools was designed to be and remained dominantly religious. A considerable amount of time was purposely given to religious subjects, the inculcation of religious values and outlook, and to religious rituals at the expense of time for secular educational pursuits. The schools' religious character was constantly visible through the priests, nuns, and brothers who, as the teaching staff, were omnipresent symbols of the authority and spirituality of the Church. Not the least reminder of the religious emphasis was their continuing responsibility to inquire of preadolescent students if they believed themselves to have a vocation as priests or nuns. Adding to the preponderant influence this educational system had in shaping the social orientation of its students was the exacting and unyielding disciplinary system supervised by the priests and nuns, who received the full and unquestioning support of the parents.[18] The parochial school was a self-contained social system from which Irish solidarity drew much of its strength.

There was and continued to be little appreciable difference between the social circumstances of staff and students. The educational attainments and living conditions of the families of both were much the same.* Consequently, there was little conflict of interests between students and faculty over the purposes of the parochial school or its regimen. Bolstering the character and authority of the system was the absence of competing intellectual interests, which were not encouraged, or really permitted, by the social status, secular values, and religious perspective of the Irish.

* In 1947 Archbishop (now Cardinal) Richard Cushing stated that "in all the American hierarchy, resident in the United States, there is not known to me one Bishop, Archbishop, or Cardinal whose father or mother was a college graduate. Every one of our Bishops and Archbishops is the son of a working man and a working man's wife."

In general, there were no educational advances of note among the Irish, and when they appeared they ran directly athwart both the general educational level of the Irish and the views of those who controlled the curriculum, both of whom shared an antipathy for non-Catholic education and culture. And although those who improved their material conditions increased in number, they were in no position to initiate a lay movement to improve the parochial school curricula. There was no acceptable niche in Catholic theology to shelter or support a cause of this kind and to which those dissatisfied with the status quo could turn for theological justification.[19]

The Irish knew no precedent giving the laity the right to question or the hope of influencing the decisions of the clergy. Indeed, it has not been until recently that they have raised the question of what, if any, influence the laity should exercise over educational policy. The Irish traditionally have felt that such authority belonged to the clergy. As Sean O'Faolin has stated:

> It is all very well . . . to say that the rise of Liberalism has declared the union of politics and theology an anachronism by pronouncing their divorce. The priest does not recognize divorce. For him the two worlds are inseparable; the kingdom of earth is but a battleground for the kingdom of heaven. . . . No *Irish* priest, for example, objects to lay-control of education on principle—there is no such theological principle.[20] (Emphasis added.)

In an interview with the author a young Irish priest offered a less abstract analysis as an explanation of the uncontested clerical domination of parochial education:

> The immigrants generally didn't have too much tradition or respect for learning, given the classes from which they came. . . . The Irish perhaps tried to give a monopoly of learning to the clerics. . . . The typical thing of American

Irish intellectuals would be, most of them, a leaning over backwards to, to Jansenism. It's usual for us—we protest too much. There's that kind of negative reaction if they've come from that kind of background.

Serious difficulties lay ahead for those who yielded to the allure of intellectual curiosity. They quickly found themselves at odds with Irish Catholic "fundamentalism," for parochial education—in conjunction with the religious cleavage, class differences, and social segregation—militated against the development of genuine Irish involvement in academic interests. Roving minds and intellectual exploration (especially in other than the sciences and technological fields) were suspect because they were identified with Protestant culture (and also because they seemed such impractical pursuits). The alternatives open to most of those with intellectual goals were few and restricting: they could abandon their interest in learning and in those who shared this interest; they could divert this inclination by turning their intellectuality to theological studies and exposition in order that Catholicism might utilize and guide their abilities; or they could leave their social milieu in order to fulfill their intellectual ambitions, which often led to a complete break—or at least very strained relations—with family, friends, community, and occasionally the Church. In most instances the last choice involved great personal conflict.

The parochial school system, in centralizing, institutionalizing, and perpetuating the values integral to Irish identity, effectively obstructed Irish acculturation. However, neither the parochial school authorities nor the Irish had any real inducement or opportunity to broaden their educational or social perspectives since society imposed its religio-class barriers. In erecting such obstacles it deprived the Irish of general occupational and leadership incentives that might have turned their interest toward broader edu-

cational, commercial, and social goals. Without sufficiently numerous practical outlets for education during the
nineteenth and early twentieth centuries, there was no
reason why an influential group should have developed
among the Irish whose concern with upgrading and broad-
ening the parochial school educational emphases might
have won gradual recognition from clerical authorities.

Their static position in the social structure precluded the
emergence of Irish pluralism and, hence, any significant
interest in educational matters. It also gave them cause to
be further resistant to academic achievement—apart from
the prominence accorded it by Protestant-American society. In Irish terms, a serious interest in gaining an education, a thoughtful concern about the quality of educational
curricula, and a propensity to elevate questions about education to a level of social importance all smacked of the
outlook of the Protestant middle class, the arch-exponents
of public education. If there were more than a few Irish
who enjoyed learning, who esteemed literature and valued
an education (how else account for the numerous gifted
Irish writers and the bookish Irish?), most Irish took a dim
view of the usefulness of education and left its destiny in
the hands of the clergy. The excerpts below, taken from
Peter Finley Dunne (writing at the turn of this century)
and from James Farrell (writing in the 1930's) illustrate
both the nature and the time span of Irish negativism in
educational matters.

Mr. Dooley, Dunne's fictional character, dryly—and
probably prototypically—bespoke the Irish view in comparing the reliability of religious and secular educational
authorities for his daily customer and conversationalist,
Malachi Hennessy. Mr. Dooley observed that:

> F'r eight thousan' years, accordin' to Father Kelly's
> count, or f'r eight thousan' millyon years th' way they add
> it up in th' colledges, th' wurruld wint without [suspend-

ers] till this modest frind of man came along with an invintion that has made it possible f'r mankind to fight th' battles iv th' wurruld with both hands free.[21]

In the course of discussing the importance of the contributions colleges had made to society, Hennessy asked: "D'ye think colledges has much to do with th' progress iv th' wurruld?" and Mr. Dooley replied, "D'ye think . . . 'tis the mill that makes th' wather run?"[22]

More obvious disdain for the educational views advocated by non-Catholics was expressed by one of Farrell's characters from Chicago's Garfield Boulevard, a solidly Irish neighborhood until the 1930's, when Negroes began to settle there. Arguing about the racial problems of this period, the liberal college student's sympathetic attitude evoked an acerbic rebuke from his brother.

> "I don't see why we should think that we're better than they are because our skin is a different color," Joe said calmly. "You wouldn't. That's what comes of reading all those books the atheistic college professors tell you to read," Jim said.[23]

This hardened outlook toward public and advanced education was in no small measure due to Irish defensiveness against the mores, values, and style of life of the Protestant majority. It was, however, partly the product of and nurtured by the parochial school milieu, the values it represented, and the social separatism attributable to it.* The parochial school system remained the institutional underpinning of Irish social solidarity until the Irish entered the assimilation process.

---

* It is noteworthy that Joseph Kennedy deliberately sent his sons to nondenominational schools as a result of his belief that this would facilitate their breaking away from the Irish community and equip them more fully and effectively to participate in the affairs of society.

REFORM: IRISH CONSERVATISM VS.
PROTESTANT LIBERALISM

Politically, the religio-class cleavage produced the same results in America it had in Ireland; simply put, the Irish supported (or opposed) whatever Protestants opposed (or advocated). The interests and values of both were so deeply imbedded in religious conflict that the *Boston Pilot* pungently editorialized in the 1840's that "co-operation for any length of time in important matters between *true* Catholics and *real* Protestants is impossible."[24] The "important matters" were so inextricably caught up in theological differences and the emotionality of religious prejudice that they could not be jointly undertaken or otherwise accommodated until the religious issue appreciably subsided. This was not to occur until the social distance between the Irish and Protestant Americans lessened and put them within social, intellectual, and emotional reach of each other—for many years.

Two issues affecting the Irish prior to the Civil War did much to exacerbate the already hostile feelings generated by the religious question. The first was the emergence of the Know-Nothing party, the culmination of the deep religious hatred of nativists who looked upon the Irish as unruly, dangerous Catholics who were neither desirous nor capable of adopting the values and sense of propriety that distinguished what was becoming the "American way of life." As Catholics, the Irish were an unwanted menace who were certain to debase the national character and destroy the national welfare.

The second issue, partly arising from the first, was that of Reform, which the Church and the Irish strongly resented. Both issues heightened Irish hostility toward Protestant Americans, who in raising these to a level of national importance drove the Irish even further from the values and style of life that were coming to prevail for the nation and which they hoped to persuade the Irish to accept.

The earliest outcries against the Irish immigrants centered on their religion, which was all the more suspect and exposed to attack because of their ethnic differences, unfamiliarity with the amenities of American social comportment, and their lowly educational and economic status. The street fights that broke out in Irish neighborhoods during and after the 1830's and the sensationalist tracts vilifying the Church were the first signs of greater religious tensions yet to come, and were followed by a continuing spate of magazine articles and newspaper editorials denouncing the Irish. The growing anti-Catholic sentiment gained new impetus from the impact of the multitude of Irish who entered the cities during the Famine Emigration, and finally crystallized in the activities of the Know-Nothings, who led the political movement to halt immigration and to ward off the menace they insisted Catholicism represented. The religious bias upon which the Know-Nothing movement was founded was revealed in Article II of its charter, which explicitly stated that:

> The object of this organization shall be to resist the insidious policy of the Church of Rome, and other foreign influences against the institutions of our country, by placing in all offices in the gift of the people, or by appointment, none but native-born Protestant citizens.
>
> You furthermore promise and declare that you will not vote or give your influence for any man or office in the gift of the people unless he be an American-born citizen, in favor of Americans ruling America, nor if he be a Roman Catholic.
>
> You solemnly and sincerely swear, that if it may be legal,

you will, when elected to any office remove all foreigners and Roman Catholics from office; and that you will in no cases appoint such to office.[25]

Even though the Irish were the object of the Know-Nothings' religious prejudice, some influential Irish Catholic voices lent the Know-Nothings a qualified approval. This paradoxical response was inspired by the scathing Know-Nothing denunciation of the German immigrants (of 1848), whom the Irish detested as immigrant revolutionaries who had fled Germany, the "infidels, foreign anarchists, and universal republicans" who were foes of the Church and advocates of the atheistic Marxist doctrine. Commenting on the Know-Nothings through the *Boston Pilot,* its official newspaper, the Boston Diocese was of the opinion that if the Know-Nothings prevented the Germans from obtaining political power in the United States, "posterity [would] look charitably over the multitude of political crimes committed by that organization of ignorance and bigotry."[26] Apostasy was more reprehensible than heresy.

Well before the political tensions stirred up by the Know-Nothings, however, the Irish had encountered another political trend which they at once regarded as anathema—the Reform Movement. The Irish had reason enough to oppose reform because its inspiration, leadership, and support were Protestant, and since among the changes the reformers hoped to effect were the life style and habits of the Irish. Despite this, Irish resistance to and dislike of Reform was rooted in their theological view of the nature of man, which conflicted with that of the Protestants.

The belief underlying the Irish Catholic view of the cause of social evils is that man, due to original sin, is fallen; as a result, he has many frailties and suffers grave hardships not susceptible of great transformation by mere mortal efforts. The assertion of will power and the exercise of reason, therefore, will not relieve the individual or society of serious problems and distress except with Divine assistance. Even then, the imperfect nature of man is such that he must inevitably suffer. Consequently, reliance upon human effort guided almost entirely, if not exclusively, by reason (upon which Protestant reformers based their efforts) to achieve such profound social changes has decidedly limited possibilities.

From the Irish point of view, the most effective prescription for ameliorating the difficulties and dilemmas inherent in the human condition was acknowledgment and repentance of sin, of error, and the hope that Divine intervention would be forthcoming in response to the prayer of the penitent seeking relief from the lot meted out by Providential design.

Coupled with their dubious view of the possibilities of Reform was the Irish resentment of "do-gooders" engrossed in attempts to redesign society, oblivious to or heedless of the wishes of those whose lives they hoped to improve.

> The Catholic Irish had an instinctive distrust of reform and novelty. The optimistic belief of advanced Boston thinkers in the perfectibility of man did not jibe with their religious creed of the constancy of the old Adam in frail and weak human nature. They had brought from Ireland the suspicion that the man who came to do good was a proselytizer in disguise and sought conversions. Their conservative traditionalism looked with disfavor on new ideas or the disruption of the old patterns. They had a temperamental distrust of the professional reformer, intolerant of standards not his own: "busy bodies," the Irish called them, "who care not so much as to ascertain what is right, as to run on their own account, without pausing to inquire whether they are sent or not."[27]

To be sure, the Irish wanted better living conditions than those they could afford or were accessible to them, but they

least of all appreciated the patronizing concern of Protestant reformers whose real interest seemed less in replacing
slums with decent housing and the amenities of life than
in bringing the Irish into conformity with their own standards and style of life. The great stress the reformers placed
on temperance and the evil of smoking made it evident that
they had no compassionate personal interest in the welfare
of individuals. Particularly ironic to the Irish was the Reform Movement's grave agitation about drinking. The Irish,
well aware of the problem of alcoholism in their midst, resented abstemious Protestants who insistently sought to
deprive them of an age-old social custom, a way of con-
viviality as well as escape.

As the Reform Movement gained momentum in the
1840's the position of the Irish grew worse, since reformers
were convinced that the Irish also opposed the abolition of
slavery and women's suffrage. They were all the more
critical of Irish resistance to the temperance drive in particular and to Reform in general, and in Massachusetts "the
failure of the enforcement of the prohibition laws was laid
at the door of the Irish, and the State Temperance Committee announced it would fight Catholicism as part of its
struggle for human freedom."[28]

In slurring as "Catholic" those Irish habits and attitudes
they judged to be in dire need of improvement, the reformers transformed a social problem into a religious dispute and vitiated the possibilities of improving the social
conditions they so deplored. And their provoking the Irish
by dwelling on the latter's social shortcomings made the
social and political distance between them ever more rigid
with the weight of their constantly growing mutual resentment. The Irish rejected and derided the ethos and ends
of Reform, thereafter regarding its causes as Protestant in
spirit and practice—and therefore totally unsupportable.
What is probably an equally severe criticism, by Irish

standards, of the goals of Reform is that they thought them
to be hopelessly impractical, a view that many still hold
today (if not entirely without justification).

Irish opposition to Reform carried over into the first
decades of the twentieth century, when they withheld
support from Populist proposals for governmental regulation of the economy, measures from which they stood to
benefit. Monsignor John Ryan, a leading Irish Catholic
activist for social reform at this time, who shared many of
the Populist views, commented on the general lack of Irish
support for reform groups, saying:

> In these [reform] activities . . . I found only a handful
> of Catholics who were prominent. Few were leaders. . . .
> Intelligent and competent Catholics were willing to work
> for laudable objectives in a Catholic organization, but
> seemed timid or fearful about associating with non-Cath-
> olics for similar purposes.[29]

There were, however, no Catholic associations that could
organize Irish support for such goals; such organizations
could only have drawn upon the clergy for leadership, and
the clergy was normally disengaged from such causes because of the conservative and separatist position of the
Church. The conditions that were to bring about a relaxa-
tion of religious animosity had not yet materialized. Nor
were they evident as late as the 1940's and later in Chicago,
where Bishop Bernard J. Sheil, a stalwart champion of social and economic reform, was an isolated voice in the
nation's largest diocese. Despite his strenuous activities
on behalf of Reform the Church's policy changed little, if
at all.

As the Reform Movement turned its energies to the issue
of slavery, the Irish found themselves even more alienated
from its ends and the social order it represented. The growing public advocacy of Abolition struck the Irish as fraught

with irony, for "Irish Catholics could not forget that Protestant preachers and 'Puritanical fanatics' who spoke so
eloquently against slavery had also said many unkind things
about Rome."[30] Notices in the papers and posters at places
of employment carrying the warning that "No Irish Need
Apply" gave the Irish good reason to feel that their lot was
not much better than that of slaves.

The Irish had strong, personal reasons for opposing Abolition. Negroes were increasingly in competition with them
for jobs in some eastern cities, and as the Civil War drew
near there were frequent outbreaks between them in these
urban areas. At times held in lower esteem than the Negroes (in Boston the Irish were called "white Niggers"),
many Irish felt that Abolition would only make jobs more
difficult to find and decided that "on the continued bond-
age of the Negro depended the salvation of the Irish. That
was the [Irish] laborer's view. Anyone who wished to liberate the slaves was no friend of the Irish."[31]

Irish attitudes on Abolition were also influenced by the
conservative Catholic view, which dealt with this issue in
much the same way and for the same reason that it coped
with social reform in general. Abolition was a goal that
should be achieved only gradually; it was not properly a
matter for political action, and least of all a legitimate
cause for war. Changes in social custom over time, rather
than concerted political or military action, would bring
about the desired result.[32] The Catholic Church in America,
highly sensitive to the grave tensions developing from this
issue, carefully refrained from promulgating an official
position to avoid exposing itself to criticism on a national
scale. In exercising this restraint it was also able to avoid
disruptive internal dissension, for the wide array of attitudes the Irish held on this question ranged from the advocacy of the continuation of the slave trade to favoring
Abolition, positions not shared by most Irish. Generally

speaking, the Irish opposed Abolition because of their more fundamental hostility toward Protestants.

In some quarters Abolition was looked upon as another indication of the radical actions of Protestant reformers whose primary interest was the destruction of the Catholic Church. Indeed, some "influential Irish leaders, especially among the clergy, associated the abolitionist agitation with radicalism in general—a radicalism which, in the United States as in Europe, might ultimately be directed against the Catholic Church."[33] In this light Catholic support of Abolition (and the Reform Movement) would have been the equivalent of coming to the aid of the devil's party.

By now feelings between Catholics and Protestants were so aggravated that no Irish voice could sway Irish convictions. Daniel O'Connell, the leader of the Catholic Association and Ireland's hero in the struggle to repeal the Union with England, called upon Irish-Americans to support the abolitionist cause in the interest of the principle of political liberty that traditionally had been so deeply cherished in Ireland. But upon commending Britain's efforts to abolish slavery, he drew sharp criticism from the Irish in the United States, who argued that Abolition was properly subordinated to their problem of securing equality from Protestant America.

In sum, certain critical events befell the Irish immigrants from the earlier until the latter decades of the nineteenth century. All sprang from and were shaped by the Catholic-Protestant religious conflict and reached their most intense pitch as a result of the massive Famine Emigration. The Irish found themselves discriminated against because of their religion and spurned as social outcasts since they were ill-educated, rough-mannered, working-class people. They came to be ideologically, because they were religiously, at odds with the reformers who had raised and popularized the political issues that dominated the nation during that century. The latter also represented the political and social styles and values that were always to hover over these newcomers as the standards in terms of which they would be judged by the dominant social strata. For all these reasons the points of conflict that developed between the Irish and native Americans carried over into the mid-twentieth century when, for the first time, the Irish were truly caught up in the process of "structural" assimilation.

In their social and ideological interests, the Irish were ill-equipped to cope with the conditions of their new life in America. Their entire history under England's domination had prevented them from developing the necessary diversity of roles and multiplicity of spokesmen who might have created the variety of attitudes and alternative actions which facilitate participation in all phases of the political process of an open society. Having lived in a social monolith, the Irish until recent decades took their cues on the dominant questions of the times from their only authoritative spokesmen—the Irish prelates and priests, whose position and influence was made well-nigh impregnable by the traditional religious hatred that consumed the Irish.

Inasmuch as the predominant interest of the Irish hierarchy and clergy was to protect the Church and maintain the faith of its communicants, they responded to religious discrimination and threats through policies of political conservatism and educational separatism. These resulted in the social withdrawal of the Irish, who became extremely defensive about their position and the values upon which it was based. And this posed a paradox for the Irish, since they were unable to transform their ardent patriotism (by which they strove to excel all others by incontestably demonstrating their identity and qualifications as American citizens) into a lever that would enable them to enter and fully participate in society.

A New Ethnocentric Force:
The European Immigrants

In the era after the Civil War large numbers of European immigrants sought a haven in the United States from poverty and tyranny, and the proximity of their communities and their competition for jobs created new problems for the Irish.

These European immigrants were as alien to and as resented by the Irish as they were by native Americans. Even though the preponderance were Catholic, the faith they shared with the Irish was least of all a common bond uniting them. Some, such as the Italians, had inherited memories of the Church in Europe at its lowest moral ebb and were far less influenced by the hierarchy and their village priests than were the Irish. Furthermore, since few, if any, of these Catholic immigrants had experienced religious persecution, they were less ardent in their commitment to the faith and less willing to acknowledge clerical authority than the Irish. Although they had a certain respect for the priest, he claimed and exercised considerably less influence over them in social matters.

The differences in languages, customs, and social styles among these new ethnic groups added to the divisiveness of their differing religious outlooks and relationship to the Church. Each group strongly desired to continue the use of its native language in the nonliturgical parts of the religious services; this generated severely strained feelings in polyglot parishes, especially in those that had Irish priests. And the subordination of the European priests to the Irish hierarchy could hardly have improved the angry feelings that had arisen between the groups.

The cultural diversity among these immigrant groups was so religiously abrasive that they resembled Protestant denominations in the variety of their religious attitudes and customs. The Italians, for example, named their churches after the traditionally revered patron saints of their towns and villages in Italy and held annual celebrations in their honor—a custom foreign to the Irish. Nor, like the Italians, had the Irish converted to Protestantism or harbored undisguised anticlerical sentiments—and still remained within the ethnic group. At least as incredible to the Irish was the National Polish Catholic Church, whose priests are permitted to marry. Unlike the European ethnic groups whose identity is not a function of their religious perspective, the more flexible an Irishman's attitude toward the Church the less Irish he is and the more socially remote from other Irish.

Still another reason for disliking the European immigrants was the American attention to the struggles waged by the leaders of certain of these national groups on behalf of political liberalism. The Hungarians and Italians, for example, had fomented insurrectionary democratic movements against the established order, and the men who led these revolutionaries, such as Kossuth and Mazzini, had openly assailed the Catholic Church and the Pope. Their efforts to overthrow the monarchies and establish democratic governments quickly captured sentiment in America, and Kossuth was even feted in the United States for one year during his unsuccessful attempt to win financial assistance for the liberation of Hungary. On the other hand, the Irish leaders who came to this country seeking aid for Ireland's fight for independence were seen by native Americans as unruly Catholics opposed to a democratic order because of their religious fidelity to Rome.

The reaction of the American Catholic Church to the struggles of the European revolutionaries was predictable. The Irish prelates and the Catholic press generally condemned these rebels and were equally bitter toward the small group of liberal Catholics in Ireland who had publicly expressed sympathy for them and their fight for democracy.[34] Rather than calling for moderate reform of these governments or lending moral support to these popular movements, the American Irish hierarchy took a staunchly conservative position and in so doing identified radical political reform with Protestantism. ". . . Catholic policy in Boston as elsewhere resolutely opposed the policies of red republicanism which, in retrospect, it linked with an atheistic plot of Protestants to undermine Catholic civilization."[35]

The Irish now faced a new and curious dilemma—they found themselves caught between the dominant strata of society and the lower-class Catholic (and Jewish) immigrants from Europe. Their resentment was all the more bitter because the nature of the Irish Catholic–Protestant American religious antipathy was not at all understood by the new Catholic immigrants. Moreover, the latter were essentially unaware of the religious discrimination the Irish had encountered and still met.

Another difference between the Irish and the European Catholics was that the latter were less hindered in assimilating by their Catholicity than were the Irish. Their "foreignness" was more a product of the gamut of their cultural differences and poverty than their adherence to Catholicism. If they did not receive the welcome hand of warm hospitality from native Americans, at least they were generally not made to feel much, if at all, less desirable than the Irish. At least, some Americans felt, the native lands of these immigrants were part of the stream of western civilization, and their customs had a quaint, appealing charm.

In contrast, the Irish had come to America as an English-speaking people who were familiar with and had adopted much of the Anglo-Saxon culture. It must have been bitter for the Irish to recognize that they were not accorded significantly higher status by Protestant America than were these lowly European immigrants. And since the Irish had been identified as the standardbearers of Catholicism in America, each succeeding generation must have been perplexed and dismayed because it was so little more socially acceptable than its predecessor. The new immigrants were first of all members of quasi-exotic nationality groups whose cultural distinctions were apt to disappear over time. The Irish, however, were first of all Catholics, and the conviction of native Americans was that this distinction was ineradicable.

LOCALISM: OBSTACLES TO ASSIMILATION

Barred from assimilating into the American middle class and pressed by strange European immigrants with whom they had nothing in common except their mean living conditions, the Irish had little real access to social outlets that would have enabled or encouraged them to establish new attachments in the upwardly mobile regions of society. Naturally seeking to live among their own kind, they became a people of the neighborhood, community, and parish, whose interests and outlooks remained local. They were partial to the affairs of the parish church and the ward—attending wakes, conversant with ward and party politics, and involved in parish social activities.

As has been pointed out, the parish church became the unifying symbol for the Irish, a constant, dominant physical presence that comforted them amidst the injustices they bore, as it reminded them of the special nature of their identity. The pastor, priests, nuns, and the parochial school were the primary agents giving social coherence to the Irish whose solidarity was anchored to the Church. They

angrily—and enviously—viewed those of the dominant society as their oppressors who lived in an entirely different
and unfamiliar world.

The confluence of all the forces subsumed in the religious conflict between them and the Protestants discouraged most Irish from yielding to the forces of assimilation.
To leave an Irish neighborhood in search of the satisfactions
and social style of middle-class living was exceedingly
difficult, since it usually meant to forsake the life style of
the working-class Irish Catholic. It required one consciously
to deemphasize the significance of religion, to enter the
occupational and social spheres of the amorphous (by comparison) Protestant world, and to adopt its social style
and tastes—all of which had for so long loomed as anathema
to Irish respect and security. With such deep reinforcing
influences for their own values and life style, choosing to
become upwardly mobile was the equivalent of a social
metamorphosis. Indeed, such thorough-going acculturation was, as the Irish perceived it, not merely a change in
their mode of life; it was almost literally regarded by them
as the equivalent of religious heresy. Pye's observation
about acculturation in a greatly different context is no less
forceful in this one.

> The power of others is . . . absolute for it is the power of
> making one willing to change oneself into their image.
> There is possibly no other circumstance in which people
> can sense more fully the human meanings of power and
> attraction than at the heart of the acculturation process,
> for this is the point at which people are giving up the most
> precious thing they have, their own integrity, in order to
> take a part of the identity of others who are foreign, with
> all that that word can mean.[36]

Of course, individuals here and there did break away
from the ethnic group and begin to assimilate. How they
did is not relevant for present purposes, but that they did is

important, for in adopting the values and life style of the upwardly mobile Protestant society they were derogated by the Irish who did not. Those Irish who "succeeded" were derisively referred to by those they had left behind as "lace-curtain" Irish,* individuals who considered themselves so vastly superior to those who had not similarly achieved that social contact between the two caused strained feelings and became increasingly less possible. The "lace-curtain" Irish, it was said by the others, were ashamed of their origins because they assiduously and ostentatiously (by working-class Irish standards) cultivated the style of life and attitudes of the social strata into which they had moved. They "put on airs," and thought themselves above associating with old friends in the old neighborhoods. In the eyes of the "shanty" Irish, as the "lace-curtain" Irish called their

* There is an interesting parallel between the Irish, prior to the time significant numbers of them reached middle-class status, and the Negroes of the past as well as of today. The vocabulary of both groups contains depreciating terms ("lace-curtain" for the Irish, "hincty" and "dicty" for the Negroes) used exclusively to describe those who have or who pretend to have "achieved." These terms have no counterparts which accord distinction or recognition to the individuals who have risen to the socioeconomic level of the dominant, but strongly resented, society. The implication for both the Irish and the Negroes has been that such success irrevocably severs one from his group because it requires "conversion" to the values of the "enemy."

The more intensely held and sharply differentiating the values, symbols, and characteristics of minority groups, the more pronounced and clearly defined are their identities and life styles. The more distinguishable such groups are from the dominant strata of society, the greater likelihood that they will be socially isolated in all but the inconsequential aspects of life. This, of course, perpetuates their different life styles. The special attributes or skills they possess which society respects, envies, or admires will not win them acceptance as equals while their fundamental differences persist, and may even highlight these differences. Distinctive vocabularies or idiomatic expressions reflect their remoteness from the mainstream of society.

detractors, these Irish *nouveaux riches* had with deliberate intention discarded a "Catholic" style of life for a "Protestant" one.

The significance of the terms "shanty" and "lace-curtain" for the "structural" assimilation of the Irish is all the more pointed in view of the fact that these terms are exclusively American in origin and use. In Ireland the vast majority of the population was Irish, the dominant ethos was Irish Catholic (except in northern Ireland), and economic and social conditions permitted extremely few to improve their status appreciably. In Ireland the persecuted comprised the overwhelming majority, who wanted to rid their country of foreign oppressors, not to discard their way of life for that of the English. To the extent that they envied the ruling class it was due to the natural appetite that all human beings have for abundance, comfort, and power, not because the English style of life was "better." The few who achieved a lofty station were usually written off for having "capitulated" to the English aristocracy and the Anglican Church.

It is also noteworthy that the terms "shanty" and "lace-curtain" have fallen into general disuse in the United States only during the past generation, the period during which ever larger numbers of the Irish (along with other ethnic groups) have come to enjoy the social and material satisfactions (and the tribulations) of middle-class living.

It is now clearer why there has traditionally been a strong anti-intellectual* disposition among the Irish who have

* "Anti-intellectual" refers to a resentful attitude toward those of real, self-, or socially imputed competence who deal with ideas and whose choice of words and/or manner differentiates them, justifiably or otherwise, from others. The anti-intellectual may have more, less, or the same natural ability as those he criticizes as "intellectuals." The term "intellectual" refers here to those who are involved in and concerned about the realm of knowledge—as creators, distributors, users, or critics who derive satisfaction from dealing with

written prolifically in defense of Catholic intellectuality and intellectual contributions. For the Irish to contribute to the main body of secular intellectual enterprise it would have been necessary to regard the secular order as one that was legitimately and, necessarily, wholly open to inquiry and criticism, and to accept philosophical differences without summarily rejecting those whose views clashed with theirs—a change that is now manifestly evident among them. Furthermore, they would have had to have shared the values of scientific inquiry, and this would have been tantamount to concurring with non-Catholics about the nature and ends of education. Consenting to this would have led to a sharing of the life style and social values of intellectuals.*

What also made it virtually impossible for the Irish to enter into intellectual affairs was the lack of a social base of support. On the one hand, intellectuals were predominantly

---

ideas. The line between the authentic and the spurious is at times a function of the fashionableness of views.

The foregoing is not to imply that the Irish have not been especially creative and prolific as playwrights, authors, and literary critics, for they are indeed well represented as accomplished individuals in these fields. The focus here deals exclusively with scholarly inquiry in the social sciences and philosophy, where questioning and research have often run athwart or questioned the interpretations of Catholic theology. In the past, Catholic authorities have effectively discouraged lay and clerical enterprise in these fields of inquiry, as the Index alone attests.

* The Irish who have begun to assert themselves in intellectual pursuits, essentially represent the vanguard of a movement that is not yet widespread among them, as the following suggests.

An Irish Catholic colleague of the author, who teaches at a quite reputable eastern university, mentioned during an informal conversation that the Irish Catholics in the city in which the university is located regard him as an anomaly. They ask, he said, "How can a Catholic be teaching in a Protestant school?"

anti-Catholic; on the other hand, the intellectually inclined
Irish could expect stern disapproval and sharp rebuke from
those Irish with whom they associated and lived.*

An Irish scholar who has candidly and deftly analyzed
the Catholic attitude toward intellectuality, as well as the
position of the Church on educational matters, is Thomas
F. O'Dea. The following observations are taken from his
excellent book, *American Catholic Dilemma*.

> . . . the development of American Catholic life from immi-
> grant origins has been complicated by the partial segrega-
> tion of the Catholic community and the partial alienation
> of American Catholicism from important aspects of Ameri-
> can secular culture.
>
> .   .   .   .
>
> This subtle marginality of ours has been the cause of
> inner conflict as well as of external difficulties. It has re-
> sulted in a subtle division of the American Catholic mind.
> On the one side is a firm identification with American so-
> ciety and strong loyalty to and love for its basic institu-
> tions. On the other is an alienation from the intellectual
> and spiritual experiences which . . . were central for those
> of Protestant background.
>
> .   .   .   .
>
> . . . the attitude cultivated in the seminarian appears at
> times to be characterized to a high degree by a kind of
> passive receptivity; the impression is given that Christian
> learning is something "finished," and that education is a
> formation to be accepted from established authority with
> a minimum of individual initiative and critical activity
> on the part of the student. The attitudes of the priest
> have an especially strategic influence on Catholic atti-
> tudes generally.[37]

* No little conflict, it would seem, was the burden of the Irish
Catholic who followed his intellectual bent. Some forsook, others
temporarily left the Church, with all the difficulties that implies for
the once committed for whom there could be few truly understanding commiserators.

World War I initially, but essentially World War II and the technological revolution that followed it, tore the Irish loose from their community-centered moorings and thrust them into the rootless, upwardly mobile society that eradicated all but their religious identity. As growing numbers of Irish moved away from their old communities and parishes into new communities whose residents had lost most of their ethnic identities through intermarriage or assimilation, the Irish were also distant enough from their ethnic milieu and the sway of the parish church that growing numbers would pursue their desire to explore and participate in the intellectual community.

The argument of this chapter has been that the social identity of the Irish in America and their position in its social structure were determined by certain conditions and events caused by the Catholic-Protestant religious cleavage and by pronounced class differences.

The next two chapters will endeavor to show how the constraints of religion and class and the Irish political heritage led to the identification of the Irish with the Democratic party, affected their involvement in city politics, and constituted the social foundation of the Irish political style.

The Politicization   5
of the Irish

During a conversation with the writer about the long association of the Irish with the Democratic party, an Irish priest said, with an air that assumed everyone took it for granted, " 'Irish-Catholic-Democrat' is a single concept." Although it is true that the Irish have been aligned with the Democratic party through the nineteenth and most of this century,* their commitment to the party has been weakening for over a generation.

The Irish first drifted away from the Democratic party because of the assistance the United States gave to Great Britain in the early days of World War II. The traditional Irish hostility toward England, perhaps in conjunction with the isolationist mood so prevalent in this country at that

* The Irish in Philadelphia and Rochester are notable exceptions to the rule, having affiliated with the Republican party to which they had access as a result of the interests of Republican party bosses in these cities.

time, was strong enough to compel some of them temporarily to withdraw support from the party or to break with it entirely.[1]

The Irish association with the Democratic party was further and seriously attenuated when the Democrats chose Adlai Stevenson, a divorced man and an ideologue, as their presidential nominee in 1952 and 1956. Concurrent with and contributing to their continuing shift in party allegiance was the prosperity the Irish had come to enjoy, which eased their movement, as property-owning taxpayers, into the Republican party in municipal, state, and national elections. Still another factor, and one of unusual importance, was the sudden emergence of Communism as an issue in national politics. Communism was invariably associated with liberalism, whose political home in recent generations has been the Democratic party, which increasing numbers of the Irish therefore found they could not support. In fact it was an Irish-Catholic Republican (formerly a Democrat), the late Senator Joseph McCarthy, who capitalized on this issue by associating Communism with the Democratic party.

The Irish continued their drift away from the Democratic party in the 1960 presidential election, when many voted for Richard Nixon rather than President Kennedy because they preferred a conservative candidate, rather than out of their concern about the possible negative reaction of the nation to a Catholic in the White House.* If in 1964 many returned to the Democratic party because they, like a number of others, found Senator Goldwater's unrealistic arch-conservatism and inconsistencies objectionable, there were still those who found him a most acceptable candidate.

For many generations, however, the Irish had been al-

* This was confirmed by conversations with a number of Irish politicians and priests.

most undeviating in their support of the Democratic party. The origin of their commitment to (what ultimately became known as) the Democratic party was as early as the last years of the eighteenth century, when the Federalists passed the Naturalization Act of 1790 and the Alien and Sedition Acts of 1798. The Federalists enacted these laws (the second opposed by Jefferson, and both held unconstitutional by the Supreme Court) for the express purpose of halting further Irish emigration to this country. Through these statutes the Federalists were the first to politicize the Catholic-Protestant religious conflict and made evident their preference to restrict the party to Protestants.[2]

In the decades preceding the Famine Emigration, the multitude of Irish immigrants who entered the eastern cities immediately encountered the resentment and then the animosity of native Americans. They soon realized, especially once the Protestant-led Reform Movement got under way, that religious and class differences had erected an altogether impregnable social barrier. It was this social impasse that forced them to turn toward the party of the "common man," although they were a curious urban counterpart to the small farmer in whose image this phrase was fashioned.

Religious prejudice, which spread into the Midwest during the 1830's and 1840's, reached its peak in the 1850's with the Know-Nothings. Despite the meteoric rise and fall of the Know-Nothings, anti-Catholic bias did not lose a political spokesman, for the Republican party at once revealed its sentiments by condemning the Irish as its "uncompromising foe," and blaming them for Fremont's defeat in 1856. On the eve of the Civil War, *Harper's Weekly*, anxiously surveying the national scene, warned that "the Irish race in the United States is very powerful, far more so than its numbers justify. It rules most of the large cities, not only on the seaboard, but in the interior also."[3]

Taking full advantage of their exclusion from the Republican party and the society it represented, as well as capitalizing on the ethos of the Jacksonian era which claimed that government was the legitimate province of the common man, the Irish surged into urban politics. Party workers, with the understanding assistance of party-appointed judges, provided swarms of illiterate Irish immigrants with instant naturalization and dispensed the favors, jobs, and other kinds of assistance that assured their political loyalty.

After the Civil War, when social and political respectability in the North were securely lodged in the Republican party, the political, religious, and socioeconomic lines were firmly drawn. The Democratic and Republican parties, representing different sides of the tracks and different churches, were in hostile opposition to each other. The Irish were to remain staunchly Democratic for approximately another century.

THE IRISH ENTRY INTO URBAN GOVERNMENT

The Irish took jobs with municipal governments for a number of reasons. To begin with, employment in the city bureaucracies was an opportunity to leave the squalor of slum and tenement living and to stake out a small measure of personal and economic self-respect. The Irish were unskilled, illiterate immigrants who desperately needed work, and the police, public works, and (as they became municipally owned) the fire departments required only manual labor or rudimentary knowledge from most of those they employed. These departments, representing the major services provided by the cities during most of the nineteenth century, afforded the Irish a degree of job security and material well-being that few had ever known and that they only infrequently found in other laboring jobs. Employment in urban government was virtually a form of social security, and also enabled the Irish, people from a sedentary peasant economy, to sink roots in the communities in which they had settled. This was a more attractive choice for many than shifting from one job to another in the cities or moving to mining towns or joining the construction companies that were building the railroads and canals leading out of the East.

Another factor was that employment in urban government, particularly after the advent of the Jacksonian era, was normally obtained through patronage appointments the political party in power controlled and dispensed. This system of recruitment was ideally tailored for the Irish during and after their rise to prominence in the urban Democratic parties, for the essential requirement of patronage appointees was that they support their benefactors at the polls. The Irish had substantial reason to give such support, both out of gratitude and concern for their jobs and because of their social, economic, and political exclusion by Protestant-Republicans.

Even before the Famine Emigration the Irish had begun to staff the ranks of the police, fire, and public works departments, and over time some rose to higher administrative posts and others won elective office. Still others sought public office directly, bypassing the bureaucracies. Through them the Irish began to establish themselves in the party by constantly increasing their share of patronage. In the course of capturing power in both Irish and other wards they gave patronage appointments whenever possible to those with whom they had the closest ties—other Irish. The political camaraderie that had arisen among them, when linked to their ethnic identity, served them particularly well in the generations after the Civil War when other immigrant groups began to demand a share of patronage and political representation in the party. By then the Irish had come to conceive of the Democratic party as their party, as an extension of their identity.

The Irish had another advantage over these later-arriving immigrants other than their familiarity with and influence in politics. During the latter decades of the nineteenth century the larger cities found themselves harder pressed to meet the needs and problems of their phenomenally expanding populations—a result of the millions of immigrants pouring in from Europe. In addition to the social problems, another was the growing need for the expansion and reliability of existing municipal services. And with each increase in the number of jobs to provide additional services, the Irish, who had political power and numerical prominence in the urban bureaucracies, were able to claim and control a disproportionate number of patronage jobs for "their own."

It was during this period, the last half of the nineteenth century, that the Irish alderman became a very important person in Irish communities, as his constituents increasingly sought him out for the advice and assistance that in Ireland the priest alone could provide. His newly won prominence did not, however, disrupt his close relationship with the priest, even though he was looked upon as one whose influence was to be reckoned with. Through the Irish politicians the bond of *Irish* Catholicism had merely extended its sphere of influence while politics flowed ever more pervasively into the lives of the Irish, the priests included.

Underlying all the reasons for Irish entry into government and their success in party politics was their ability to speak English fluently when they arrived in America, and their extensive familiarity with the institutions, processes, and laws of Anglo-Saxon government. Instead of struggling with a language handicap for at least one generation after their arrival, the Irish were able quickly to accustom themselves to their new environment, adjusting with relative ease to the social and governmental terrain. They could at once understand the order, explanation, advice, or admonition of a policeman, judge, or administrative functionary, and were at first more familiar with the nature and functioning of municipal government than any other aspect of American urban living. Sheriffs, bailiffs, police, and courts were old acquaintances in a new setting.

Although they were very likely unaware of it, the Irish were far better equipped, through class, personality, and political experience, than native Americans to build and master powerful urban political organizations. Certainly their experience in maneuvering around and manipulating the law stood to their advantage. Of equal importance, however, was their relationship to people. As Shils has noted,

> the nativist leaders have almost without exception been characterized by their inability to organize an administrative apparatus for their movements, or to hire or attract others to do the work for them. The organization of an administrative apparatus involves a minimum of the capacity to trust other individuals and to evoke their trust and affection to an extent sufficient for them to pursue the goals set by the organization or its leaders. American nativistic-fundamentalistic agitators have lacked this minimum of trust in even those who share[d] their views.[4]

These qualities are far more often found among those of the working, rather than in the middle or upper, classes.

The foregoing general explanation for the affiliation of the Irish with the Democratic party and their entry into urban government leads us to an examination of the social system through which the Irish were recruited into urban government and the party; of how politics became so ingrained in Irish life; of certain similarities in organization

and operation between the Catholic Church and the urban
Democratic parties; and of politics as a form of Irish alienation rather than a means to upward social mobility.

THE INVOLVEMENT OF THE IRISH IN URBAN POLITICS

The *involvement* of the Irish in urban politics must be
distinguished from the fact that so many of them have
been employed by municipal bureaucracies and held public office, for political involvement connotes an aspect of the
Irish way of life—not merely that they had occupations in
city government and identified with the Democratic party.

A salient feature of the Irish mode of living was their
preoccupation with local politics, a characteristic initially
explained by the nature of their political experiences in
Ireland. Although rendered powerless by the English, the
Irish were ever striving to obtain some relief from their
oppressive conditions, and every Irishman looked forward
to the day when Ireland would be free. In one way or
another, the Irish were continually involved in political
affairs that gave them considerable exposure to local politics. In contrast with the immigrants who came to America
after them, the Irish had a very distinctive political culture,
composed of specific and deep-seated attitudes about the
means and ends of government, attitudes whose legitimacy
was reaffirmed as a result of their experiences with Protestant America, the Reform Movement, and the Know-
Nothings.

Once settled in the urban areas, the Irish capitalized on
their political skills and knowledge which, in addition to
their status and social exclusion, gave them access to the
menial jobs in city government and prompted them to enter
local politics in the Democratic party. Political power,
which had been invariably used at their expense, now be-

came their quest, just as issues were their anathema. In this context the Irish social structure took on its American form, and in the process urban politics was woven into it as an elemental component. Two institutions that figured prominently in the politicization of the Irish social structure were the saloon and the police department.

The Saloon

Accompanying the growth of Irish communities was the appearance of many saloons, most of which were owned by the Irish. The saloon was the "poor man's club," the one social center available to the innumerable poorly paid Irish workers for whom it was the most popular, perhaps the only, place where they could learn the important news about the parish, jobs, politics, and Ireland. The saloon was a congenial, lively place where people could indulge themselves in idle gossip and argument and find a respite from the drudgery of work as well as from the duress of life and its onerous responsibilities.

The saloon proprietors were very important figures in the Irish communities. Their status as entrepreneurs and their business success elevated them to a position that was both recognized and enhanced by their acting as "officials in the church societies, marshals in church processions, [and] chairmen in church meetings."[5] Some became actively engaged in politics and organized the Irish into clubs that provided them with a local base from which to launch political careers. Others used their influence in the community to win favors from officials in city hall. Politicians instinctively recognized how helpful tavern-owners could be in support of their candidates, as the following recollection by a Chicago ward committeeman illustrates:

> Years ago, before what was called the regular [Democratic] organization, politicians would go to the corner

saloon and the saloonkeeper was the doctor, lawyer, banker—and that's where a candidate would go on Sunday to meet the people of the community. He spent so much money in the saloon and then the saloonkeeper would be predicated [sic] over the forces in the neighborhood in passing it along because they didn't have meetings or transportation to meetings.

Oldtimers, not only Irish—Italians, and all the others—would borrow money, come in for advice. The bank was at 63rd and Halsted. People wouldn't go there on the average—they'd borrow money from the saloonkeeper. The politicians would—a fellow running for office would make ten to twenty of these different spots. It was his way of campaigning.

As growing numbers of Irish were drawn into party politics through patronage appointments, it was inevitable that politics became a major topic of conversation in the saloons, as elsewhere in the Irish communities. And because the saloon-owners' economic interests and local influence brought them into proximity with politicians, it was wholly natural that they should act as liaisons between the latter and their constituents. In fact there was a precedent for this kind of relationship in Ireland, where, as Arensberg has shown,

. . . the pub . . . was the countryman's metropolitan club. The man who worked it was a friend and kinsman, one of one's own kind. Near-urban prestige made him a superior, as one in touch with seats of power, fashion, and law. . . .

Thus, the shopkeeper-publican-politician was a very effective instrument, both for the countryside which used him and for himself. He might perhaps exact buying at his shop in return for the performance of his elective duties, as his enemies charged, but he also saw to it that those duties were performed for the very people who wished to see them done.[6]

For many years the saloon was as important a link in the communication process of the Irish social structure as was the parish church. These were the basic social institutions in Irish communities, the instrumental internal agents reinforcing Irish solidarity. It was through them, as places for socializing, that politics was integrated into the Irish social structure.*

As the Irish took over positions in the party organization, the party (and later the government) assumed the creature-comfort functions and services formerly provided by the saloon-owners to the people in the neighborhood. By this time, however, the saloons had fulfilled their role in the politicization of the Irish, and politicians no longer found them useful as recruiting and campaign centers. Then, too, as the Irish improved their standard of living and became more independent in meeting their material needs, the saloon became exclusively a place for socializing, albeit one where politics remained the most popular topic of conversation. Where else could Mr. Dooley have held his political seminars with Mr. Hennessy?

* An unknown academic who read this in manuscript form objected to the emphasis given the political significance of the saloons in Irish communities. He argued that the saloon was a natural gatheringplace for many immigrants, all of whom experienced the disabilities of the unassimilated lower class. Thus, the local politicians simply took advantage of this fact by using the saloonkeeper as an intermediary in soliciting votes. This is true, but it is not the point at issue.

Saloons in *Irish* communities were important because they were where the Irish talked ward politics and parish politics, and much less so because Irish politicians sought votes there. That they did so, however, merely increased the already considerable significance of the saloon among the Irish, as the text has suggested. They functioned to feed back politics into the Irish social structure and to align it with the Democratic party, roles they have never really played in the lives of other ethnic groups.

With the general improvement in living conditions the saloon became the tavern and then a bar, and since World War II it has gradually ceased to serve as the place where party workers and politicians gather to exchange information about local politics. Since the gradual dispersion of the Irish throughout the urban areas and into the suburbs, the tavern caters mainly to older residents, immigrants, and to other Irish after wakes. On St. Patrick's Day they are joined by college students seeking a moment of merriment and a glimpse of the past. Here and there, precinct captains drop in at those that remain (and there are fewer each year) after ward meetings. In better neighborhoods taverns tend to succumb to the middle-class urge to remove such unsightly blemishes that depress property values and the character of the community.

The Police

So many Irishmen have joined and so many are now in the police departments of the larger cities* that it is worth exploring both their close relationship to party politics and how they infused Irish life with politics.

The Irish acquired a deep respect for and envy of the power, authority, and status that the policeman's uniform represented in their unending and unhappy encounters with the law in Ireland. There, the policeman's uniform was the symbol of both the helplessness of the Irish peasants and the nearly omnipotent powers of the landlord, the aristocracy, and the Anglo-Saxon government. As late as

---

* As of October 1964, the Irish staffed a minimum of forty-one of the seventy-two highest administrative positions in the Chicago Police Department.

  Chicago has had thirty-five Police Commissioners (prior to 1923 the position was Chief of Police; it is now the Superintendent of Police) since 1861, of whom a minimum of twenty-one have been Irish.

the turn of this century constables were still sent by landlords to evict Irish peasants unable to pay their rent, and
to destroy their meager dwellings to prevent their moving
back once the police had gone. The policeman in Ireland
had a measure of authority and security that the people had
never known.

The Irish who joined the police force in the United States
sought all the satisfactions denied them in Ireland—the
status conferred by the uniform, steady employment, and
the power that otherwise lay in the realm of fantasy.

> Former Chicago Police Commissioner Timothy O'Con-
> nor once explained . . . why so many Irish have joined the
> police force, down through the years. Lacking capital,
> often the victims of prejudice, they sought security. "In
> the old country they were denied the right of self-expres-
> sion, so the one thing that every man that was a migrant
> craved was security. Security in his mind existed in two
> ways—the ownership of property or a Civil Service posi-
> tion. So they became either firemen, policemen, mailmen,
> or entered some other branch of government or municipal
> service."
> There were other reasons, too. They had carried from
> Ireland a deep respect for the station of the policeman.
> He wore a uniform, he was part of the government—he had
> status. As the Irish became more and more prominent in
> politics, they were in a position to dispense the plums of
> patronage. And a job on the police force frequently was
> one such plum.[7]

These were tough men whose experience or heritage had
given them a great thirst for power, for in Ireland they had
always been the opposition, the prey of the police, those
who were evicted, taxed, seized for questioning, imprisoned, even killed by the law enforcement authorities. To
be able to take jobs on the police force in the very cities
where they met so much religious prejudice was an un-

paralleled opportunity that doubtless gave the Irish a deep, wry sense of satisfaction.

The Irish politicians who had established themselves in ward organizations or otherwise won the support of strong local followings knew of the effectiveness with which the English had used the police to quell disturbances and to secure their power. They were acutely aware of the intimate connection between the police and government authorities, and took full advantage of their influence over appointments to the police department to bolster their base of power.* So long as politicians controlled the appointments to the police force, the Irish policemen realized that their job security depended upon success of the party slate at primaries and Democratic victories on election day. Consequently, they, their families, and their friends were voters upon whose consistent and full support the Irish politicians could depend. Of perhaps greater importance was the ease with which the police were frequently able to influence voting in working-class neighborhoods by determining who was permitted to enter the polls. Those who were denied entry as well as those who fled without voting because they were physically threatened or actually abused[8] had no recourse except to smolder in righteous indignation. The Irish controlled the police department and frequently, if behind the scene, city hall as well. And they had not forgotten how expertly English landlords had fixed elections.

The Irish policemen exercised wide discretion in apprehending violators—and upholders—of the law. They interpreted the law with the latitude and flexibility appropriate

---

* The process through which Irishmen were recruited for the police force was much like that described by a Chicago Irish politician about a much more recent time. He said:

"My brother applied for a job as a policeman with McGuire. McGuire is in charge, and my brother had met him once or twice before. McGuire said, 'your father worked with my father, your

to their interests and those of the politicians they served, and the political morality they inherited justified this practice. As Wibberly has depicted them,

> the Irish were natural police material. They settled points of law directly, sometimes with tolerant humor, sometimes with fists as big as hams. They didn't believe in cluttering up the courts with petty arrests. The Irish policeman believed himself the law. His court was the sidewalk or the waterfront and his jury his fists. The system worked remarkably well.[9]

Where ward politics still thrives the relationship between the Irish police and Irish politicians remains a close one. As an Irish politician remarked with casual candor:

> It may sound heretical or bad government, or right out of Clausewitz or somebody, but the police departments are local branches of the war department. They are a tool of policy.

When that policy is primarily concerned with the maintenance of the party and its ward organizations (and where they exist it is), the police are closely involved in ward politics, the scene most familiar to Irish politicians. Thus, in addition to acting as the law enforcement agency for the entire community, the heavily Irish-staffed police departments have had the special function of maintaining the strength of the ward and district organizations. Nominally, the police department was the law enforcement agency for the entire city; in practice, however, it had the special responsibility of assisting Irish politicians to secure their political power.

The police departments of the urban areas have been so

---

grandfather and my grandfather worked at the _____ station, and you'll make one helluva policeman.' "

A more detailed account of the role of the family in the Irish political recruitment system is found in the next chapter.

extensively staffed by Irishmen down through the years that the policeman of the popular American image has been and continues to be an Irishman.* Hollywood films, particularly through the 1930's, and even later, have captured (and perhaps helped to create) this image by featuring such Irish actors as Pat O'Brien, James Cagney, Thomas Mitchell, Lloyd Nolan, Dennis Morgan, and others as the commissioners, inspectors, captains, lieutenants, detectives, sergeants, and patrolmen. They have usually been portrayed as warmly generous and helpful toward children, kindly toward the elderly, quick to assist the pedestrian, the *bon ami* of the neighborhood, and both fearless and determined in their pursuit of dangerous criminals.

Although the Irish policemen have exhibited such virtues in the fulfillment of their duties, the films scarcely ever pictured them dealing with the knotty moral problems involved in the determination and dispensation of justice. And Hollywood almost never touched on the intimate and important relationship of the Irish policeman to the Irish politicians in city hall.

With the many other Irish in other municipal departments, but far more influential in the Irish communication process because of the authority of their uniform and their much deeper involvement in party politics, the Irish policemen did much to establish politics as a vital part of the Irish identity. Furthermore, their authority gave them greater access to the priests and politicians, thus linking politics ever more closely to the Irish communities. In their homes and neighborhoods they discussed what most preoccupied them—the problems of law enforcement and the news of party politics. Largely because of them politics,

* As recently as 1962, Richard Dougherty, an Irish writer, drew upon the Irish for the major male characters in his book, *The Commissioner,* a novel about New York City's police department in whose administration he had served.

which was so integral to their daily existence, became the unifying secular influence among the Irish. And the police were the most visible bureaucratic symbol of the impact of the Irish on municipal government.

THE INFLUENCE OF THE CHURCH ON IRISH PARTY POLITICS

There are some interesting parallels between the organization of authority found in the Catholic Church and its parochial schools and the urban Democratic parties that took their form and character under Irish leadership. Although it cannot be incontestably demonstrated that the former in fact were responsible for the development of the latter, certain similarities between the two are sufficiently striking to merit comment.

A formal part of the religious training of Catholics, particularly in parochial schools, has been an explanation of the purpose the Church serves and of the appropriateness of the hierarchical ordering of authority it has adopted to fulfill this purpose. In America, as in Ireland, the priests thoroughly inculcated in their parishioners the Catholic dogma—the salvation of the soul as the ultimate end of man over which the Church, through its prelates and priests, has absolute stewardship on earth. The flow of religious authority begins in the parish church and continues in an uninterrupted hierarchical pattern to Rome, a system of ecclesiastical authority that has been presented as requiring the undeviating respect and obedience of all Catholics. As a result of the religious discrimination they suffered both in Ireland and the United States, the Irish have been drawn closer to the Church and the clergy than any other Catholic group. They have been the group most committed to the fundamentals of Catholic doctrine heard constantly reiterated in church and in parochial school, just as they have been those who most respected and were least inclined to challenge clerical authority or to argue for departures from the status quo.

Until Pope John XXIII called for a reconsideration of the Church's policies on the major social issues of the day, the Irish prelates and clergy have traditionally counseled patience and perseverance as the recourse for communicants dissatisfied with the Church's views or inaction. Ecclesiastical authorities have maintained exclusive control of the right to propose, initiate, and implement policy changes of whatever degree of importance; they have also excluded lay influence over personnel appointments and changes. Communicants have been relegated to the role of attentive, uninfluential spectators who have passively heard the hierarchy's promulgations and watched the intermittent struggles for position in the parish and diocese, where it was taken for granted that the parish priest who docilely waited for his position to improve waited in vain. It was the capacity to govern the parish and discharge administrative duties—to exercise authority—that commanded the attention, respect, and recognition of diocesan authorities.

The Irish became constant witnesses to the ways in which parish authorities wielded power when the Church established parochial schools. And the ubiquitousness of the Church made it all the more influential in view of the scant opportunity the Irish had to experience the varied uses of power elsewhere in society. Recalling the omnipresence of the Church's system of authority, an Irish politician said:

> The parish system had discipline built in. When the Sister took a whack at you, you deserved it. The Irish priest backs up the Sister, right, wrong, indifferent. And if I complained when I got home, my father would whack me again. The Father, pastor, curate, are very important at grammar school—a man's in charge.

> Again, with the system, you're always trying to beat
> it. At _____ University you had to be in at 10:00 P.M., no
> drinking, and no cars. . . . We used to go out the window
> just to go to _____'s to show that we could beat the
> system.

Much like the Church, the urban political organizations
that the Irish have controlled excluded party workers and
voters from a voice in policy and personnel matters. These
were determined by party officials who, because the party
organization was not self-contained like the Church, occasionally made their choices with the interests of campaign contributors and other influentials, and occasionally
the public, in mind. In recent times, of course, both the
party organization and the Church have tended to make
concessions to their respective publics whose more solid
middle-class footing has encouraged them to be more
strongly and confidently assertive, a stance they were
hardly able or inclined to assume in generations past as
members of the working class.

Party discipline, based upon a hierarchically structured
party and a patronage system, has been the lever Irish
politicians have used to bring warring factions into line,
to chasten the errant and disobedient, and to suppress or
effectively discourage most of the independent candidacies
of those impatient and ambitious to attain elective office.
The slate of candidates chosen by party officials for elective office and the compromises they have arranged for the
choice patronage appointments usually have been accepted
by those who are active in the party. An Irish politician in
Chicago recognized the futility of challenging, as well as
the wisdom of accepting, the party's decision to support
another person for a nomination he had hoped to win several years ago. In discussing the incident he stated:

> I was really bitter when I didn't get the nomination for
> _____ in my district, but I never thought of running as an

independent any more than I'd think of jumping over the
moon. Even though I'd been offered money to do this, I
wasn't going to run without the organization. . . . The value
of the organization is more important than personal values.

So is the value of the Church.

The influence of the Church on the structure of the party
organization is also suggested by the organization of the
Catholic Association. The Association, it will be remembered, was the only large-scale, widely based Irish political
organization that Ireland had known, and both its popular
support and lines of communication were based upon the
parish churches. The urban Democratic parties that were
organized by wards or districts culminated in a party central committee, reflecting the Church's local orientation
and its centralization of power in the diocese.

Moynihan, in writing about the Irish in New York City's
politics, has suggested that they fashioned the party structure in the image of the social system of the Irish peasantry,
arguing that adventurism was absent from each and that
a stable, unchanging order was their most notable characteristic.

Instead of letting politics transform them the Irish transformed politics, establishing a political system in New York
City that, from a distance, seems like the social system of
an Irish village writ large.
   The Irish village was a place of stable, predictable social
relations in which almost everyone had a role to play under
the surveillance of a stern oligarchy of elders, and in which,
on the whole, a person's position was likely to improve with
time. Transferred to Manhattan, these were the essentials
of Tammany Hall.[10]

Inasmuch as the sedentary status system of the Irish village was one in which one's claim to position was based
solely on age, this system could only have ingrained a sense

of haplessness and forced patience in the eldest sons. They alone inherited the small family plot and hearth upon the death of the father or when he yielded his position due to senility, weakness, or illness. In this system there was no competition for power, nor did the elder's status contain influence worth mentioning. He was the monarch of a hovel and a sparse piece of ground that too frequently failed to yield enough for base subsistence living. Apathy and unrelievable poverty were the fruits of this social system, not a desire to compete for power.

It seems more reasonable to suggest that the omnipresence of the Church and its system of authority, the secret societies and their comparably stern disciplinary requirements, and the Catholic Association whose *modus operandi* was based upon the parishes had a far greater influence on the organization of urban Democratic parties than did the village proprietary system. At any rate, the latter lost its influence when the Irish settled in the slums of the cities, where the pace and character of urban living uprooted the status system of the small, dormant villages in Ireland— but not the organization of the Church.

The Church and the party organization had other common attributes. Each confronted the Irish with sharply defined power structures and authority relationships, and provided them with services they could obtain nowhere else. So long as the Church and party fulfilled these responsibilities the people had no occasion to question the legitimacy of their authority. Since these were the only organizations with which the Irish had contact and to which they had access, each reinforced the character and correctness of the other. For example,

> . . . when Al [Smith] was seventeen, the St. James Union had a dispute with the priest, who had made an unpopular demand upon the club. Smith urged his friends to give

in; if they were a part of the Church, they had to submit
to it. For without authority and direction there was no
order in life.

The same went for politics. "When the voters elect a
man leader," one of the boys later explained, "they make
a sort of contract," although "it ain't written out." They
put him there to look out for their interests, "to see that
this district gets all the jobs that's comin' to it." In return,
they agree to be faithful. If "he spends most of his time
chasin' after places in the departments, picks up jobs from
railroads and contractors for his followers, and shows himself a true statesman," then they are bound to uphold him.
Otherwise they are justified in rebellion. They may "up
and swat him without being" put down as political in-
grates.[11]

The reciprocal relationship that existed between both
the priests and politicians and the Irish can be carried a
step further. Just as the priest has been available to his
parishioners at any time of the day or night, so has the
precinct captain been generally available to his voters to
help them out of various kinds of predicaments. Admit-
tedly, the precinct captains are less needed as their voters'
standard of living improves, but a comparable situation
holds true for the Church as well. The independence and
security of middle-class living inclines individuals generally to be less reliant upon the clergy for advice or assistance to help resolve their difficulties.

Irish priests gave their parishioners ample opportunity
to witness their political skills. The pastors invariably dealt
with any problem that affected the interests of the parish,
having no obligation to consult members of the parish before acting. An incident such as the successful intervention
of Father William Dorney on behalf of his Irish parishioners
during the Chicago Stockyards labor dispute at the turn of
this century and his persuasiveness in obtaining the compliance of the Bridgeport tavern-owners to close their

bars during Mass were, if not typical actions by a priest, certainly not regarded as objectionable or even questionable. As an Irish politician said of them with warm admiration, "priests are the best politicians there are," and added that

> the relationship of the priest in the parish to the people is similar to the ward organization. Your political training is in the parish. There's more politics in the parish than in the city. Someone is always vying for some position, although there's no money in it.

When informed that the author had interviewed a number of Irish priests as well as Irish politicians in preparation for this book, an Irish Catholic colleague quipped, "What's the difference?"

The parish church was associated with ward politics in yet another way, since for a number of decades it was an important link in the recruiting process for the ward politicians. The close contact between the priests and politicians enabled the clergy to obtain patronage jobs for parishioners who then became party workers. Securing employment for them was an organizational, as well as a humanitarian, concern of the priests, for unemployment in the parish curtailed the amount of the parishioners' donations upon which the church was dependent. Irish priests had an interest in the welfare of the party apart from their ethno-religious preferences. Every intercession they made on behalf of their parishioners strengthened the ties of politics, parish, and religion, the bonds of Irish solidarity and identity.

POLITICS AS ALIENATION

Since the impact of the Jacksonian era, the dominant strata of this nation have typically held in disesteem those who, like the Irish, have intentionally sought careers in politics. The span of decades during which the waste and corruption of the spoils system became the urban equivalent of national economic exploitation was all the more grievously regarded when contrasted with the brilliant contributions of the Founding Fathers, the outstanding ability and statesmanship of many members of the Federalist party, and the more illustrious of the Jeffersonians. Even more bitter was the Protestants' loss of political power to the urban masses who, in the eyes of the former, were bent on destroying the quality of life in the cities.

This gradual transfer of power necessarily bred animosities, for the immigrant Americans who made their way into urban government had a conception of the functions of government and a political style that contrasted glaringly with that of the middle-class native Americans whom they had ousted. These newcomers to American city politics thought of government first as a source of badly needed jobs, and also enjoyed the satisfaction of holding political power and the status that it vicariously conferred on so many of them.

Their interests were initially material, and inasmuch as considerations of quality had never really entered their lives, it could scarcely be expected that they would exhibit a concern about the quality of the government services they provided or the work they performed. Their style of politics, mirroring their style of life, was a rough-and-tumble struggle for survival in which the spoils of office were means of sustenance as well as legitimate rewards— not merely a corrupt and unconscionable use of material and human resources.

The middle- and upper-class Protestants, who had been so prominent in giving government its direction and tone in the early days of the nation, were aghast at the ugly grubbiness of the Irish immigrants who had captured public offices and who staffed the urban bureaucracies. Their ill-mannered, rough ways were deplored by the upper strata, whose understanding of the purpose of government was based on a belief in the existence of an interest of the entire community, be it city, state, or nation.* By this standard the advancement of narrowly personal and selfish group interests was to sacrifice the polity and degrade the nature and conduct of governmental affairs. Compromise, temporizing, power struggles, and the like could only have the most adverse effects on the public welfare. The problems of government should be settled according to the rule of reason so that "politics" would not interfere with or affect their resolution. Conducting the responsibilities of government in this way, of course, required the services and abilities of men whose comportment was gentlemanly and whose views of government were both governed by reason and cosmopolitan in scope.

This view of government, the political ethos of Protestant Americans, lost its dominance when those who shared it either lost or abandoned their influence in government to the working class. Nevertheless, their standard persisted despite the transformation of the character of urban government by the new masses, for it was affixed to the status of the most dominant social strata and was upheld over time through the activities of the reformers. It continued as the criterion in terms of which both the most and least blatantly self-seeking politicians ultimately sought to justify their actions, however distorted their reasoning. During a resurgence in the latter decades of the nineteenth century, it recaptured much of the sway it formerly exercised over local government, its influence expanding with the growth of the middle class which took up and sustained its

* This section draws on Edward C. Banfield and James Hugh Wilson, *City Politics* (Cambridge: Harvard University and MIT Presses, 1963), chap. 11.

advocacy. The more than 1700 city managers in American cities today and the penchant for nonpartisan local government in a great many municipalities and suburban communities are evidence of its contemporary strength.

In view of this, avowedly to be engrossed in the drama of city politics; to regard it as an attractive career; to be committed to partisan politics; to enjoy the tempestuousness and color of campaigns and the struggle for position and patronage; and to be attentive to ward interests—all flaunted the political standards of middle-class Protestant America, which considered these aspects of "deviant" political behavior.

Politics attracted the working-class Irish-Catholic-Democrats for almost every reason but those deemed legitimate by middle-class Protestant-Reformer-Republicans. The Irish swarmed into the interstices of the urban bureaucracies and sought and won elective offices with the most pragmatic and highly personal motivations: they wanted the income and security that municipal employment provided; were excited by the personalized election contests and intra-party factional struggles; revelled in the highly partisan and raucous campaigns; were the "insiders" close to the seats of governmental and party power who were the first to hear the choicest political rumors; and possibly most important of all, they had the deep, abiding satisfaction of knowing that they had fought for and won political power which brought them, if begrudgingly, the status of political equality from those who otherwise despised them. Excluded as undesirables from the other major arenas of society, the Irish had with continuing success invaded and entrenched themselves in city politics, for them the most exciting of all sectors of urban life.

Still, their achievements in politics were not wholly to their advantage. For the many years that politics was to be a dominant interest and important occupational avenue for them, reflecting and reaffirming their divergent social norms and style, they would remain alienated from society. Because of the Catholic-Protestant cleavage, the political morality they inherited, and their experience with the reformers, the Irish, instead of using government to create policies to improve the conditions of life for themselves and others of comparable circumstances, used their power to enhance their political position by increasing their fund of patronage and concentrating on winning elections. In so doing they symbolized the alienation of the Irish Catholic in a Protestant society. Perhaps of all the immigrant groups that have entered American city politics, the Irish most nearly fit Pye's generalization:

> Both the drama and the mechanisms of politics can attract people, engrossed either consciously or unconsciously, in all manner of personal concerns which cannot in any way find their solutions in the enactment of any particular public policies. Politics can give legitimacy to feelings of aggression and hostility, and a cloak of virtue to sordid motives. Politics can also provide the excitement of creativity and the sense of comradeship to people who have long felt themselves suppressed and isolated.
>
> People who come to politics out of such motivations will not be satisfied with the realization of any particular goals of public policy; for them the meaning of politics is to be found in the drama of participation, in the excitement of controversy and the security of association, and above all in the reassurance of being superior to others. For such people, one alternative of public policy can be quite as satisfying as another.[12]

That politics was an expression of the social alienation of the Irish can be illustrated by a detailed description of their understanding of the essence of the electoral process and the primary responsibility of the government official. The following is from Edward Ross', *The Old World in the New,* which although written in 1914—nearly seven decades after the Famine Emigration—still has validity, if diminished, for the Irish.

> In their eyes, an election is not the decision of a great impartial jury, but a struggle between the "ins" and the "outs." Those who vote the same way are "friends." To scratch or to bolt is to "go back on your friends." Places and contracts are "spoils." The official's first duty is to find berths for his supporters. Not fitness, but party work, is one's title to a place on the municipal pay-roll.
>
> .   .   .   .
>
> A genial young Harvard man who has made the Good Government movement a power in a certain New England city said to me: "The Germans want to know which candidate is better qualified for the office. Among the Irish I have never heard such a consideration mentioned. They ask, "Who wants this candidate?" "Who is behind him?" I have lined up a good many Irish in support of Good Government men, but never by setting forth the merits of a matter or a candidate. I approach my Irish friends with the personal appeal, "Do this for me!" Nearly all the Irish who support our cause do it on a personal loyalty basis. The best of the Irish in this city have often done as much harm to the cause of Good Government as the worst. Mayor C., a high-minded Irishman desiring to do the best he could for the city, gave us as bad a government as Mayor F., who thought of nothing but feathering his own nest."[13]

The opportunity to enter urban government through the Democratic party was irresistible; politics provided the Irish with the means of acquiring the self-esteem otherwise denied them and won for them a reckoning from their social adversary. Politics also proved an avenue through which alienation was broadened as it pervaded their lives. The extent to which the Irish were absorbed by and given to politics is made abundantly and graphically clear in Edwin O'Connor's *The Last Hurrah,* a novel reputedly based upon the Irish in Boston's politics. O'Connor's portrait of the Irish viewing government and elective office as their natural enterprise, as though government was an Irish team to which all, or nearly all, Irish owed allegiance, is a reminder that an American novel so immersed in politics could have been written about no American ethnic group but the Irish, and by no one but an Irishman.

James Farrell, another Irish author, illustrates how deeply politics was interwoven in the Irish way of life in his novel, *My Days of Anger*, in which political metaphor uniquely enters the introspections of Danny O'Neill, the main character. Danny's conscience tells him:

> According to Saint Augustine, even infants sinned. If he [Danny] lived to be eighty, he would have to burn in Purgatory for centuries and centuries, provided he escaped Hell. In fact, the longer you lived, the longer you would burn in Purgatory. Last night he dreamed that his conscience was a *State's Attorney grilling him in a criminal court. Conscience was the State's Attorney of God.*[14] (Emphasis added.)

The appearance of the superego in political allegory was possible only because, as an Irish alderman put it, "politics was in the air"—it was an elemental part of Irish life. The following is a wonderfully natural account from *Plunkitt of Tammany Hall* of how fully politics had entered the lives of the Irish. Plunkitt, reminiscing, said:

> I think of an old Irish woman, widow of one of Charley Murphy's lieutenants, on whom I called with a friend early one evening in 1930. There she sat at the dinner table, with her daughters-in-law and four sons. Grown men, one was a detective, one a bartender, one a horse-player, and one a lawyer. . . . The conversation, directed with great gusto and good humor, by the old lady, bore on *the same subjects that engross a district boss*. Gossip about friends, advice to one to call on a sick old woman in the hospital, an ad-

monition to intercede officially on behalf of a boy arrested
for petty thievery. Smooth the way for someone's naturalization; see that Mrs. O'Brien's boy gets a job in the Department of Sanitation. "And, you, Joe, did you go to Mass
Sunday? Did you get to confession? Oh, you rascal you,
what a lot of sins you have to confess!" She went on like
this, never saying anything sinister or evil. No criticism
of anyone associated with the Hall passed her lips,
or at least none for their public offenses. But she expressed
her contempt for captains and district leaders who were
unkind to their wives, and her sympathy for those whose
children were not a credit to them. This is the way bosses
talk when they are with their families.[15] (Emphasis added.)

This recollection contains the basic Irish interests—politics and religion—and vividly describes the manner in
which politics flowed completely into the Irish family. Of
her four sons, three (the detective, lawyer, and bartender)
were directly or indirectly associated with politics.

Excluded from society because of their religion and class,
the Irish took employment with municipal government and
identified with and captured power in the urban Democratic parties. However, although politics enabled the Irish
somewhat more effectively to present themselves as bona
fide Americans in the midst of a society that excluded them,
it also had the effect of enhancing their ethno-religious
identity and social alienation. Urban government became
their preserve, an Irish occupational enclave that gave
sharper focus to their presence and social separateness because of their commitment to the Democratic party whose
base of power was the indigent electorate. For that matter,
their affiliation with the Democratic party became the secular equivalent of their commitment to Catholicism.

. . . putting the brand of "apostate" on the Catholic Irish
who left the Democratic party set up the same response of

automatic feelings of betrayal in the mind of the devout Catholic Irishman as did the terrible word "informer" or the renegade from the Church. The word "apostate" took on a political as well as a religious meaning.[16]

Further heightening their identity and alienation was their particular use of the governmental powers they won. In Irish terms, the chief objective of government was the furtherance of their most pressing needs—power, which they had never known, and jobs, for which they had come to America. Their political style, therefore, sought to maximize their power by negotiating with their competitors and dealt with only those policies that would influence the electorate to support them. It was also developed, in part, out of their confrontation with the reformers, whose dedication to issues and policy-making caused the Irish to draw away even further from that phase of politics for which they lacked both inclination and interest.

For most of their history in the United States, politics has been a vital aspect of the Irish social structure, as important to their identity and way of life as was Catholicism.* Just as the Irish envisaged themselves as the most loyal and devout of American Catholics—as those who alone and without appreciation had waged the struggle for Catholicism in this country—they also regarded themselves as the most loyal and hard-working of all Democrats,

---

* It is worth noting how little interest the Irish have had in politics when resident in a foreign Catholic country in which their mobility is unrestricted. Dr. Sean O'Heideain, the former Irish Consul in Chicago, remarked during an interview that "the Irish don't touch politics in Argentina," where he had served.

For that matter, the Irish in Ireland have scarcely shown the interest in politics characteristic of the Irish in the United States. In the decades since World War II Irish Catholics have failed to win the mayoralty race in Dublin when Briscoe (Jewish), Dockrell (Protestant), and Briscoe won office at three successive elections.

the vanguard of all the ethnic groups that joined the Democratic party decades later.

The involvement of the Irish in party politics is partly attributable to the influential roles of both priests and tavern-owners in Irish communities. Their close relationship to politics enabled them to serve in the Irish recruiting process for both the government bureaucracies and the Democratic party. The parish church and the tavern, the only institutions serving as social centers in Irish communities, reinforced Irish solidarity and infused politics into Irish life.

The generational involvement of the Irish in politics suggests the question, "Why have most Irish not used the wider social exposure of politics as a stepping stone to upward social mobility, as have other ethnic groups in the Democratic party?" The answer is found in the uniqueness of their identity; that is, the role of the Irish politician was, except for that of the Irish priest, the one most representative of the fundamental Irish values—Irish-Catholic-Democrat-politician. Consequently, it was even more difficult for the Irish politician to forsake the ethnic group in favor of American middle-class living than for the Irish intellectual to break away to join non-Catholic confreres with whom he at least had a compelling common interest. The Irish politician was also constrained by the fact that if he openly and deliberately abandoned his special identity his political career was ended, for even if the majority of his constituents were not Irish, most of his political associates were. And if they shunned him he had no one else to whom he could turn.

The foundation of Irish identity and solidarity was composed of *Irish* Catholicism, a working-class status and life style, and allegiance to the Democratic party and engrossment in local politics—all confronted by and in direct conflict with the norms and social characteristics of Protestant-

Republican middle-class society. Inasmuch as the Irish party affiliation was a function of their religion and class, and since of these two the one most susceptible to change was class, the attrition of class differences between the Irish and Protestant Americans would weaken the Irish attachment to the Democratic party and moderate their religious attitudes.* It would also facilitate the "structural" assimilation of the Irish leaving them with the identity of American Catholics, with all the social diversity, anonymity, and uncertainty that this identity implies and contains.

In the course of moving into the middle class by adopting, becoming accustomed to, and enjoying its variety of social and economic values, the traditional Irish interest in politics has diminished for many and induced some to become involved in the issues that non-Catholics had heretofore essentially monopolized. In recent years, for example, Irish Catholics (priests, nuns, and laity) have not only openly and militantly allied themselves with such liberal causes as the civil rights movement, but the traditional voices of liberalism within the Catholic community—*The Catholic Worker* and *Commonweal*—have found a larger Catholic audience with a serious desire to liberalize the Church as well as society. The very fact that *Commonweal*, the Catholic intellectual journal, recently judged Ingmar Bergman's, *The Silence*, among the best films of the year after it had been condemned by the Catholic Legion of Decency[17] is impressive evidence that a plurality of views, increasingly independent and assertive, has emerged

---

* In Chicago, at least, there is no longer the strong animosity between the more affluent Irish Catholic businessmen and the Masons and Shriners. In the recent past Irish businessmen have joined these fraternal orders for business purposes, and non-Catholic members occasionally invite Irish Catholic friends to their more important social functions.

among Irish Catholics,* as well as in the larger Catholic community which has long been under the conservative influence of Irish clerics.

Such incidents highlight the disintegration of the Irish social monolith, a trend already well under way through ethnic intermarriage, the absorption of the Irish into society's now greatly varied occupational structure, and the diminution in religious animosity. Thus, as the Irish have gained acceptance and esteem (nearly everybody marches in the St. Patrick's Day parade) and come to experience social and intellectual diversity, they have simultaneously begun to disappear. Increasingly they have memories and nostalgia in place of an ethnic identity.

* According to one informant, in recent years the most liberal voice for change within the Catholic Church has been young, very devout, and visionary Irish Catholics. Some of them visualize the Church as *ideally* being national in the use of language in all parts of the service, and with each national church having great discretion over local policy-making. Rome would then unite the Church much as the British monarch unites the Commonwealth nations.

Chicago's Irish Politicians 6

This chapter concentrates on the Irish politicians, past and present, in Chicago's Democratic party for the purpose of confirming the major points presented in the preceding chapters. A considerable part of this chapter deals with the Irish "political style," which, in addition to focusing on certain distinctive Irish social characteristics in a political context, also partly accounts for the unusual success the Irish have enjoyed in party politics over the years. In addition, the nature of *Irish* Catholicism is described, as is its relevance for the ethnic identity and political solidarity of Irish politicians.

Although it is argued that the analysis generally holds true for Irish politicians in the northern and eastern urban areas, one important qualification must be mentioned. That is, Chicago's extremely well-organized, ward-based, and patronage-supported Democratic party has acted as a forceful organizational focus for and constraint on the attitudes, norms, and behavioral traits of Chicago's Irish politicians. Elsewhere, in the absence of party organization or where weaker party organizations existed, the integral components of the Irish political style more easily yielded to the attrition of social change—except, perhaps, where the Irish were directly confronted, as in Boston, by Anglo-Saxon Protestant society.

THE IRISH ENTRY INTO CHICAGO'S DEMOCRATIC PARTY

The Irish were the first large Catholic immigrant group to settle in Chicago, where they comprised the bulk of the work force that built the canal, constructed the railroads, and provided most of the manual laborers in the stockyards and in the railroad freight yards. The first and largest Irish community developed around the stockyards —in Bridgeport and Canaryville (in the Eleventh and Fourteenth Wards). Other Irish moved to western sections of the city as canal construction neared completion, and still others later formed communities on the Northside and in the southeast section of the city near the steel mills, where St. Patrick's and St. Kevin's parishes are located. By 1850 the Irish accounted for twenty per cent of Chicago's population.[1] As their living conditions improved, the Irish moved to new neighborhoods in the southeast (Hyde Park, Woodlawn, and South Shore), south (Garfield Avenue), and southwest (Beverly Hills and the area encompassed by the Eighteenth Ward, where incoming Irish until recently settled when reaching Chicago).

The "Southside" Irish (the Stockyards area) were the vanguard of those who joined the ranks of the municipal departments and became the motormen and workers for the privately owned streetcar companies whose ownership the city later assumed. They were greatly assisted in obtaining patronage jobs by the Irish politicians who had won elective office and control of the Democratic ward organizations in the Irish and other sectors of the city. So quickly did the Irish establish their dominance in the party that by the 1880's the Democratic party in Chicago was popularly referred to as "Mike McDonald's Democrats." The political strength and involvement of the Irish in the next decade is indicated by their preponderant control of the ward organizations, each a stronghold of votes and of patronage.

> [In the 1890's] the city was made up of thirty-five wards and practically each of these was under the complete domination of a single man, or of a small group whose word as far as the choice of delegates was concerned was supreme. [Among those who controlled the wards were] Charlie Martin, Billie O'Brien, Johnny Powers, Mike McInerney, Stanley Kunz, Billie Loeffler, Steve Revere, Jimmy Gray, John McGillen, John Colvin, John F. O'Malley, Billie Lyman, Tom Byrne, Tom Gahan, Maurice O'Conner, Joe Duffy, Alleck Jones, Tom Cusack, Mike McDonald, Mike Doherty, Bathhouse John Coughlin, Dick Gunning, Tim Ryan, Ed Cullerton, Mickey Ryan, Joe Mahoney, Jim Dailey, and John Brennan. . . .[2]

Of the twenty-eight persons named, twenty-four were Irish.

Even as the great influx of European immigrants vastly expanded Chicago's population, the Irish retained firm control of a far higher percentage of party and elective offices and patronage than their proportion of the population entitled them. Of the 104 aldermen who represented both parties in the city council from 1908 to 1910, nearly one-third were Irish. In 1926, when nearly all the European ethnic groups far outnumbered the Irish, thirty-three of the fifty ward committeemen* were Irish, and they held a

---

* The ward committeeman's office was established by statute in 1923 and since that time has been the real seat of power in the ward-based party organization. With rare exceptions, the committeeman has selected the aldermanic candidate (legally a nonpartisan office) and frequently has chosen himself.

similarly disproportionate number of patronage positions.[3]

If in gradually diminishing numbers, Irish preeminence in the Democratic party has continued essentially uninterrupted through the intervening decades, very likely reaching its zenith during the administration of Mayor Richard J. Daley, which began in 1955. In 1962, twelve of the fifty aldermen and twenty-one of the fifty ward committeemen were Irish,* even though estimates (there are no reliable statistics) give the Irish only approximately 350,000 of the nearly three and a half million residents in Chicago.

It is now appropriate to describe the process through which the Irish established their hegemony in Chicago's Democratic party.

POLITICAL RECRUITMENT: FAMILY AND FAMILY REPUTATION

The Irish politicians and administrators interviewed by the author entered politics "naturally" rather than as a result of "rational calculation" or chance. That is, the Irish social environment had so thoroughly blended politics with their lives that a political career (in either elective or appointive office) has been as laudable and desirable an occupational goal for the Irish[4] as finance, commerce, the professions, or the arts have been for those from other ethnic and social groups. Furthermore, seeking a position in government through both personal acquaintances and the party has been as standard (and inviolable) a procedure for the Irish as the civil service examination is today the typical recruiting procedure for those in quest of most jobs in the federal bureaucracy (where, even when qualifi-

* In this same year, a conservative estimate showed that of the seventy-three assistant state's attorneys, thirty-two were Irish.

cation has been demonstrated, personal contacts are not a hindrance to appointment).

The highly personalized, informal character of the Irish recruiting process is highlighted in the following responses to the question, "How did you happen to go into politics?" The answers make it evident that the Irish became politicians for the same reason that many others have become engineers, salesmen, doctors, or businessmen—they were, as one said, "born into it." In answer to this question a ward committeeman said:

> My father was a precinct captain in the precinct I live in now. He went to meetings and took me with him. I liked it. I went to a lot of those old-time parades.

Another remarked:

> It all started out with my grandmother, who was an alderman in _____, Illinois, and who was also on the school board. My grandfather was a school superintendent, and my father has held several offices.

An administrative official employed by the State of Illinois and an official in the party in Chicago, said:

> You'll enjoy this. My grandfather was a police captain, my father was a police lieutenant, four uncles were in the police—one was a chief of the detectives, one a lieutenant, two were sergeants, and I have two brothers who are policemen and a sister who teaches.

An alderman replied:

> I got into politics in a natural fashion. My dad was in politics before me. He was the committeeman of the _____ ward. I was always interested in the activities of my father dealing with the people in the community. I was aware of politics long before I could vote. When I was a kid in school I was in charge of keeping ward headquarters clean in order to make spending money.

The late John Duffy, who was successively an alderman, committeeman, chairman of the Finance Committee of the Cook County Board of Commissioners and then its president, said:

> I was born and reared in politics, at Fifty-Fifth and Halsted, south of the old Stockyard district. In my early days it seemed that everyone, particularly boys at fifteen and sixteen, got interested automatically in politics. Everyone in the neighborhood did.

These comments are typical of the extensive familiarity of the Irish with ward politics prior to their pursuing political careers, and of how early and easily politics filtered into their lives. They were informally drawn into politics through family, relatives, and friends who held office or patronage appointments and for whom political affairs were interwoven in both their vocational and leisure interests. In fact it has been just these kinds of relationships that have produced "political families" among the Irish in Chicago's Democratic party.

In Chicago there are quite a few Irish politicians who are of the second, and several of the third, political generation —among them the Clarks, Sains, Cullertons, Ryans, Sheridans, McMahons, and McDermotts. For the most part, their political power has been very real within the sphere of influence of the ward organizations, offices, and patronage they have controlled, and the lineages they represent have personalized and enhanced the traditional eminence of the Irish in Chicago's Democratic party. In addition to serving as important symbols of individual achievement for the Irish in general, these persons have also helped establish the image of the party as an Irish party. This, in turn, has helped temper the Irish factional struggles for power within the party and acted as a unifying influence in the face of challenges from other ethnic groups. The successes of the latter in winning a greater influence in party slate-making and a larger share of patronage has been attributable to the votes they commanded or through the great personal skill of a man like Cermak, rather than as a consequence of Irish ineptitude or disunity.[5]

The achievements and renown of these and lesser political families have also helped maintain the prestige of politics among the Irish, which partly explains why they have continued to regard employment in government (and its corrollary, activity in the party) as an attractive occupational avenue. Perhaps even more significant is the fact that they point up the function of the Irish family and familial associations as vital components of the social network—of which the Irish political recruiting process is one aspect, and upon which it has been heavily dependent in bringing reliable Irish into government and party office.

The political recruiting and tutelary roles played by Irish families in general (remembering that administrative and elective offices are of equal importance in acquiring familiarity with ward and party politics) were described by an Irish official who has held several political appointments in the city and county (Cook) governments. His knowledge of the relationship of the Irish social structure to political recruiting is sufficiently intimate and detailed to warrant quoting at length.

> Reilly knows Moran from the old neighborhood. He is now responsible for the nurture, feeding, and schooling of Moran's son. This is the protegé [sponsorship] system. It's never nepotism. An outsider would see young Moran's appointment as nepotism because he's the son of Moran. But although he is, and [even though] I'm the son of a policeman, inside the ranks [of the Irish] we're both responsible [to our mentors].

Each generation ties into the previous one. All right, so I don't know Costello. But my cousin is married to Moore and he knows Costello. The matter is of no cost to Moore, but he has to say [to Costello], "He's my kinsman, give the job to him," on the basis of my grandfather and my father [having known Costello's grandfather and father].

But you can't put a chucklehead in as a big man. Therefore, subconsciously, you do it this way—as his father, if I'm in charge of his development I won't be as objective about him, so I'll have a friend of mine take over as his teacher. I want to stress that these ties do an "idiot" absolutely no good. If you asked me now, "Would your cousin be good as the Superintendent of Police?" I'd say, "No, leave him where he is." You've got to be realistic about these things.*

As they consolidated their position in the party and were increasingly confronted with the problem of maintaining their power, Irish politicians had to assure themselves of

*This practice of bringing new blood into the party and into government office is sharply criticized by those who believe that the demonstration of competence through a merit examination should be the only criterion for admission to public service.

Whatever grounds justify a criticism of the patronage system or an ethnic patronage system, it should be realized that this process is not unique to party politics. Its counterpart exists in the business world, where sons frequently follow their fathers into individually owned enterprises of which they ultimately assume ownership, and in large enterprises where friends and relatives frequently assist young men in securing positions. In such situations, family, class, religion, and personal obligation continue to compete effectively with competence as standards of employment.

Efficiency and ability have been values stressed by the commercial world of middle-class Protestant society with which most Irish have had little meaningful contact till recent years. Not having adopted these values and having come to feel that the Democratic party was "theirs," "their club," it is perfectly natural that the Irish have relied upon those standards of recruiting that have best served their political interests and with which they have been most familiar.

the reliability of the Irish they recruited for most, and especially the more sensitive, patronage appointments* and elective offices. Just as the Irish who controlled ward organizations had to recruit precinct captains who could be relied upon to deliver votes for the candidates the committeemen supported, the Irish party officials needed assurance that those Irish officials slated for city and county offices would support the party's decisions and would be generally dependable. In addition, individual Irish politicians needed some basis for judging the reliability of other Irish politicians with whom they were unacquainted.

The reliability of the Irish who entered the party's ranks was crucial from yet another standpoint. As other ethnic groups settled in Chicago they soon developed a taste for political recognition and began to win from the Irish a measure of representation on the party slates and a growing share of patronage. But because their interest in political power centered on employment opportunities and the status political position would confer on "foreigners," and since they were competing with the Irish rather than with Protestant-American society (which they were more anxious to join than were the Irish), the Irish realized these groups could not be expected to place party interests above their ethnic or individual aspirations. As the "cosmopolitans" in the Democratic party who were finding themselves ever more pressed by these "parochial" foreigners from Europe, the Irish felt that they alone could act responsibly for the fundamental interests of the party.

The most practical and effective criterion the Irish could

---

* "Many of the positions in the fire and police departments depend on reputation. There are places which are very confidential, where you have to depend upon someone. Malone's an example. He's been appointed to the _____ and I know that's one of the reasons —because they knew him for what he was. It's happened in many departments." From an interview with an Irish alderman.

use in recruiting other Irish upon whom they could depend
was the standard in general use among the Irish—family
reputation. Among the Irish a man's *moral* reputation was
determined by whether or not he was a good Catholic,
which essentially meant that he had to keep his faith with
the Church and observe (at least outwardly) marital fidelity. The preeminent *character* attributes by which a man's
reputation was assessed were his decisiveness* and loyalty,
traits that were held as vital to tests of social aggressiveness
and accomplishment as they were respected in the keenly
competitive arena of party politics. Individuals who best
exemplified these attributes were, *ceteribus paribus*, most
apt to rise in the ranks of the party. However, an immediate
advantage was held by those who could refer to the reputation of a father or relative whose reputations were known
to those who had to make snap judgments of character
when dispensing patronage to strangers or when supporting appointments of others personally unknown to them.

Family reputation has been and continues to be an important standard used by Irish politicians to assess both the
potential of those seeking to enter politics and the performance of those in politics. As a committeeman commented:

> When I was first a candidate for alderman I got hun-
> dreds of phone calls and contributions because people re-
> membered my father. They'd say, "Are you _____
> _____'s son? Okay, I'll be for you." Regardless of ability,
> there is an inheritance I had of tremendous importance in

* An instance of an Irish administrator losing face among other
Irish politicians because of his indecisiveness and "weakness" occurred during a difficult situation that arose in a committee meeting.
The other Irish politicians expected him to resolve the matter de-
cisively and with neat dispatch. However, he attempted to pass this
burden along to them. One of the latter said, "He could have taken
the heat but he passed it along to the _____ Commissioner
[Irish], and then said to him, 'You can take care of me on this, can't
you?' [The Commissioner] answered, 'sure, we'll take care of you!' "

my campaign. I had at least thirty to forty per cent of my
original success due to the reputation of my father locally.[6]

A city councilman discussing the relevance of reputation
for political appointments, remarked:

> Reputation has a definite effect on what decisions you
> may make with regard to giving a young fellow a job.
> Mr. X or Y, if I know X's background or family and am
> certain Y's present qualifications are better, Mr. X will get
> the job. I think that problem is another phase of the nature
> of Irish politicians. On the surface they may seem to be
> fighting among themselves all the time, but there's a deep
> sense of loyalty to old friends and neighbors.

Officeholders also benefit from family reputations.

> There is an Irish judge here who goes further in politics
> because of all the Irish politicians who dominate the scene
> here. They recognize what a great fellow and leader his
> father was.

Family reputation not only has been an influential factor in
staffing the party and government offices, but it also affects the severity of the punishment exacted for ineptitude.

> There was a case where a fellow [Irish] was in trouble.
> His uncle had been a prominent politician, and he [the
> nephew] had a job with a responsible position and some-
> one was out to get the job because he was in trouble.
> Now they could have discharged him or given him a break,
> and they gave him a break because of the reputation of his
> dead uncle.

Nor is the influence of reputation from beyond the grave
inconsequential. It carries no little weight even when two
Irishmen are seeking the same office, as the next account
makes clear.

> Houlihan's son was in the police in charge of detectives
> in the _____ Division. Casey's son was in another branch,

and when a good deal came along Houlihan always asked
for Casey. But Captain Connors [who worked with Houli-
han] wanted somebody else, and Powers [who worked with
Connors] would always say "no" to Connors. He'd say,
"Casey's clout [sponsor] is Houlihan's father. And Connors would say, "Houlihan's been dead for twenty years."
And Powers would say, "I know."

If our fathers worked together and if I've never met you
before—even though I've never met you before, I know you.

Even patronage appointments of trivial importance and
outside of the Irish talent pool may hinge upon the reputation of a deceased Irish politician. An administrator told
this story about such an incident.

A Negro came into ward headquarters, a fellow that
I'd never seen before. Well, there are eighty guys like that
a night [looking for patronage jobs], but I listened. Then
he said, "I'll take anything, I'll cook." I asked him if he
could cook and what experience he had, and he told me
he'd worked on the railroad and then for Mr. Shaughnessy.
I asked which Shaughnessy, and he said, "Mr. Tim Shaughnessy [a prominent Irish politician in a large eastern city
who died a few years ago]. I cooked for him at his home."

This guy really cooked for Tim Shaughnessy! If he was
good enough to do that he's okay, and he's now back at
the _____ District.

While reputation is important among Irish politicians,
they can be indifferent to their reputation among non-Irish
politicians.

Nothing is worse than an Irishman with a bad reputation. I don't care what [non-Irish] lawyers think about me.
If you're Jewish or Italian or something else and asked me
for a continuance and the next day I said, "You didn't call
me"—well, it's okay as long as it's stupid politics. But if
you're Irish and asked me for a continuance and I said,
"You never called me," you might see me in court and say,

"You're a goddamned liar—but never mind!" Actually, you'd walk out and tell everybody [other Irish politicians] and then I'd be anathema wherever I went.

We [the Irish] get very involved in these things. One of _____'s biggest problems is a breach of ethics with _____ [both of whom are Irish officials in a state office].

Even though an inherited reputation is an initial advantage to any Irishman entering politics, it is not possible merely to draw on its capital.

There's one caveat—you must live up to all the legends [about your family] and have no weakness. If you tell me to watch the door and I leave, my name is mud in big letters. My name will flash through the grapevine and I won't be able to get into the washroom at City Hall. This is not to say that charity won't be extended, but the idiot son is always the washroom attendant, the other is the county commissioner.

THE IRISH POLITICAL STYLE*

The social characteristics that impart uniqueness to the Irish political style are deeply rooted in the perspective and history of the Irish as an alienated working class. These characteristics are: a deeply genuine and abiding interest in people as distinct individuals; a political morality with distinctive attitudes toward both political means and ends; a near-clannish definition of and concern about political loyalty (especially vis-a-vis other Irish politicians); and a predominant interest in political power.

These characteristics are elemental components of the ethnic identity the Irish developed under England's rule

* Political style is defined as one's general manner of acting in politics, a distinctive behavioral quality imparted by attitudes and values of primary importance.

and were reinforced by their formative social experiences in the United States. As these characteristics gained a defined focus in party politics they were integrated into a style. Their contemporary viability is a measure of the extent to which most Irish politicians are separated from the social style of middle-class Protestant America, a social distance that is no less real despite having diminished appreciably.

Class: "Of the People"

Some of those who write about politics tend to forget that it is about people. The Irish never do. Since their political style is derived from their close experiences with people, it is useful to examine this relationship further.

Irish politicians have an obviously genuine and highly personal interest in people, though not a marked concern about the welfare of people en masse. Their interest is in the specific individual, in particular people who live in their neighborhood, precinct, or ward, and for those who come to them for assistance. Their feeling for people and the real personal satisfactions they derive from helping them stem from the deeply rooted feeling they have of being "of the people," which is in visible contrast with the milieu of middle-class Protestant society. Still strongly resistant to certain aspects of the life style of the upwardly mobile, the Irish "like people and like to be liked. They'd rather have a big wake than a lot of money. They like to have a lot of friends. . . . That's the trick in politics."

The authenticity of the Irish orientation toward the particular individual and their lack of interest in remedying society's ills through social welfare measures is made evident in the words of a councilman who observed:

> One of the things about the Irish being sentimental, they like to help somebody get along. They're more interested

in personal assistance than in putting legislation through. I get more satisfaction out of individuals getting—helping individuals [rather] than getting some big idea across in the city council or awakening the public conscience. I never did that. I might get some satisfaction from that, but I don't believe I would.

Indeed the Irish distinguish the two parties in terms of their contrasting attitudes toward people.

Republicans are more fakers, so-called do-gooders, re- formers. They insult the intelligence of the average man and woman. That's one of the reasons for their downfall. They feel that they don't have to render a service to the people as long as they have the media. . . . They always are trying to picture themselves as people living in an atmos- phere of self-righteousness. They're as undesirable as any- one else. The Democrats realize they're not perfect, not the best, that anything can happen to human beings.

Even those Irish who rise to the most powerful positions in government are sensitive to the basic interests of the people, as the following comment about Mayor Daley makes clear.

A Democratic civic leader was impressed by Mayor Daley's "clean-up campaign" and said, "watch these pros— a guy like Daley who wanted to keep the city clean . . . the first thing after he was elected. If I'd been Mayor of Chicago I wouldn't have thought of that first. I probably would have thought of some urban renewal project. That shows how down-to-earth he is. He knows what the people want. He lives with the people. . . . And some of these guys [civic leaders] are so highfalutin' they don't know what the people want.[7]

Some may skeptically discount the authenticity of the Irish politicians' expression of concern about the problems of others, preferring to believe they must render service in return for electoral support. Although the Irish (and all

other) politicians are ever-mindful of the relationship between assistance rendered and votes on election day, it is
equally true that the Irish do "understand, know, and like
people. The Irish like each other, have a lot of fun, and
really like people. . . . But when you do business with any
of them it's because you like us or we like you—or we don't
do business at all."

Class Constraints

The deeper significance of the Irish politicians' involvement with people is best visualized by noting the class
norms that the Irish politicians most respect and carefully
observe. These norms derive from a much earlier period in
Ireland and were given renewed strength as the Irish became alienated in the United States, when there were no
"lace curtain" Irish upon whom the vast majority of
"shanty" Irish could heap their scorn and resentment.

Although these norms have less constraining influence
as the currents of assimilation more completely envelop
the Irish with each passing year, they still exert no little
effect on most Irish who desire to rise, or have risen, in government and in the party. The strength of these norms continues to obtain because politics remains an exemplary field
of endeavor among the Irish; therefore, Irish politicians
must especially exemplify these norms to maintain status
among themselves and among the Irish upon whose good
will they are at least partially dependent.

The net effect of these norms is to prevent social distance, and its concomitant invidious distinctions, from appearing among the Irish politicians. This is achieved by
their tacit agreement that visible signs of upward mobility
are prohibited. To assure themselves that economic attainments will not change their social style (and thereby jeopardize their political position), Irish politicians take par-

ticular heed of the symbols of the class constraints most important to the Irish: an inconspicuous residence, social style, style of dress, and a common manner of speech. A graphic illustration of the first is revealed in the next comment.

> Some time ago there was a rumor circulating that [following his election as mayor] Richard J. Daley was moving from Bridgeport [where he had lived all his married life]. The reaction among the Irish was, "Well, of all the nerve!"
>
> Martin Kennelly [whom Daley defeated in the 1955 primary] lost support [among the Irish] when he moved into the Edgewater Beach Hotel. The Irish say that you may forget who you really are and who really put you up there when you think of moving away from where you've always lived.*

As the prototypical Irish politician until more recently, Mayor Daley felt compelled to remain where he had lived for many years instead of moving into another home and residential area more appropriate to his position as mayor by nearly any standard—except the Irish. Indeed, most Irish politicians who have substantial incomes either remain where they have lived all their lives or live in better homes that are undistinguishable by their exteriors or interiors from others in their neighborhoods. The Irish are conspicuously inconspicuous.

This holds with equal force for their unwillingness to participate in the social world of celebrities and socialites.** It would not be merely gauche, it would be repre-

---

* By contrast, Jacob Arvey, one of the party leaders during the Kennelly administration (1947-55), was referred to as "Colonel Arvey of Lincoln Park West and Miami Beach."

** Senator Robert Kennedy is far more the Irish politician than was President Kennedy, whose associates were much more diversified than his brother's. For example, an article written about the

hensible for Irish politicians to permit themselves to be drawn into the lively, colorful, and affected whirl of these social "pacesetters." A fuller enjoyment of the material satisfactions society affords is not to be confused with the indulgent, ostentatious life of socialites and social climbers whom Irish politicians shun.

> Take Daley and those aligned with him who are constantly together at wakes and on street corners [talking to people]. First, the Irish save face among themselves. To be a cheap whore and get in a celebrity column or be seen buying drinks for a Hollywood actress—you'd lose votes on that basis.

Apart from Mayor Daley, whose personal and political interests have transformed him into a highly celebrated public figure with a manifest interest in status,* there is almost literally no mention whatsoever of Irish politicians

---

Senator when he was U. S. Attorney General described him as follows:

"He is motivated—in his concern for friends and allies, in his almost emotional refusal to be swayed by wealth and social position, and in his pugnacity as well—by a stern and literal belief in concepts of good and evil . . . and by a sense of duty to family and country. . . ." *Life Magazine,* January 26, 1962.

Such a figure as Jimmy Walker (former Mayor of New York City) was, quite obviously, an exception to this and nearly all other rules observed by Irish politicians. He was a style-conscious celebrity who had no power in the party by which he was used and which depended upon his swaggering personality to attract broad popular support.

* Mayor Daley's serious concern to modernize Chicago and to improve the image of City Hall and the Democratic party has necessarily involved him in status considerations. Greeting national and international dignitaries and making speeches in more fashionable circles have been typical of his activities in the past several years. Such status demands on his time have placed him in the role of the "transitional" Irish politician who is the link between the old and the new Irish. See Appendix B for an elaboration of this point.

in any of the media that does focus not exclusively on political affairs, and there is little of that. They are still very
much concerned about being recognized for observing the
style of life that views upward mobility as suspect, at least
—perhaps especially—if outward signs are a necessary mani-
festation.[8] Old customs live on.

> The toastmaster at a banquet held several years ago
> was Pat Hoy, and everybody who was anybody was at the
> speaker's table. Arriving late came Richard J. Daley. He
> looked around the room and said, "There certainly is an
> elegant group here tonight, the finest, most prosperous
> Irish in Chicago. I can't help but think of your mothers and
> fathers and grandparents who would never have been
> allowed in this [Conrad Hilton] hotel."
> This set the thing back into its proper perspective. There
> was an uproar of laughter. Then he said, "I want to offer
> a prayer for those departed souls who could never get into
> the Conrad Hilton."

Another symbol of class constraint among Irish politicians, albeit one which has lost importance in the past several years, is their style of dressing. That is, except for those
whose status interests have superseded the ethnic constraints, the Irish politicians' clothing in no way singles
them out from anyone else. Those who, ostentatiously or
otherwise, wear more expensive and stylishly tailored suits
are never regarded as models of sartorial elegance by the
Irish. In general, Irish politicians prefer to be inconspicuously dressed and are uninterested in stylish clothing.*
However, they are extremely alert to the motives such
garb reflect in politicians from other ethnic groups whose

---

* A colleague who read this in manuscript remarked that the
observation was equally true for the Irish in New York City politics,
and added that "at the state conventions all the Irish wear blue
serge suits and a dark tie."

wardrobes are visibly expensive and obviously stylish. As a county administrator commented about an Italian city official:

> Take _____. He's the hope of the Italians, but he's getting "fat." He wears white-on-white silk shirts. I told him to wear a seventy-dollar suit instead of those two-hundred-fifty-dollar suits he wears. He's trying hard [to impress others].

The income of the Irish politician is not to be used for the kind of consumption that would be deemed elementary by those who desire to join the upwardly mobile. In fact, Irish politicians who have large incomes usually have enjoyed it quietly and, in contrast with the standards of the middle class, frugally. Otherwise they are open to severe criticism by the Irish.

> When the Irish get together and are talking about another Irishman who's made a lot of money [and lives ostentatiously] you'll hear them say, "I wonder how much of it he stole. I hope he gives some of it away before he goes to Hell." Why you take Parky Cullerton or Daley, or some others, they are all independently wealthy, but to look at them you'd never know they had money.

The general disdain of Irish politicians for the few among them who are highly income and status conscious, especially when these interests compete with their demanding party and government responsibilities, was expressed about two such "deviant" (upwardly mobile) Irish officeholders and party officials. The comment was made about one that "he's no longer with the Southside Irish. Those of the Irish who are interested in money are usually regarded as a bunch of bums." The individual about whom this comment was made described his interests in life as follows:

> I'll tell you honestly I could have had other [political] positions, but I wouldn't give up my business. It all de-

pends upon what you want out of life. I like to have time to myself, time for my family, and to go hunting and fishing, and to spend some time at my country home. . . . Others think that power and prestige are more important and are worth the price. I don't feel that way.

Of the other "deviant" Irish politicians, the remark was made that the Irish politicians who know him "consider him a two-dollar thief."

The gulf that still exists between the outlook of the alienated Irish Catholic working class, in which the Irish politicians' values concerning the uses of material comfort are imbedded, and that of the middle class, is still keenly felt by Irish politicians.

> The Irish can't wear wealth well—it might be embarrassing to be doing these things [living according to middle-class standards] because of friends in the lower economic levels who may be thinking about them and they would feel uneasy.

Political parlance is as crucial to the Irish political style as are its material manifestations, and the Irish studiously avoid pretension, verboseness, and phraseology not characteristic of the common man. Plunkitt's advice to politicians is as pertinent to the Irish today as when he first offered it:

> . . . Some young men think that the best way to prepare for the political game is to practice speakin' and becomin' orators. That's all wrong. We've got some orators in Tammany Hall, but they're chiefly ornamental. You never heard of Charlie Murphy delivering a speech, did you? Or Richard Croker, or John Kelly, or any other man who has been a *real power* in the organization? Look at the thirty-six district leaders of Tammany Hall today. How many of them travel on their tongues? Maybe one or two, *and they don't count when business is doin' at Tammany Hall. The men who rule have practiced keepin' their*

tongues still, not exercisin' them. So you want to drop the
orator idea unless you mean to go into politics just to perform the skyrocket act.[9] (Emphasis added.)

Observations by several Chicago municipal officials expressed much the same sentiment in a more contemporary
setting:

> We are of the people, number one. Have you met any of
> us who have gone to Ivy League schools? Our families,
> our people, don't believe in exclusive education. We be-
> lieve in a separate kind of education—still, to be part and
> parcel of everybody, living with the boobs. Being at a
> factory gate would be an emotional trauma for a Newton
> Minow.

> .   .   .   .

> Something you keep at home is what you've read. The
> trappings of the intellectuals, poetry readings—I doubt if
> at checkers and the I. Q. test they can beat the group at
> the Fourteenth Ward.

> .   .   .   .

> At a city council meeting Smith said, "Only one thing that
> describes this meeting is a quotation from Cicero," and he
> spoke it in English. Nolan got to his feet and said, "Alder-
> man, what you've just said loses something in the trans-
> lation from the original. Do you know the original?" Smith
> said, "No." Nolan did, but he wouldn't go around talking
> about it.

Irish politicians are extremely critical of those with a
penchant for speechmaking in the council meetings, holding that this is normally irrelevant except for the legitimate
purpose of succinctly explaining one's position on a particular measure that has been reported out of committee.
There is, in the opinion of the Irish, no need for a councilman to make speeches if he has attended the committee
meetings where he can air his views and make cogent comments if he has thoroughly studied the bill. Consequently,
the Irish regard those who use council meetings as a forum

for expressing their position on bills as publicity-seekers, persons who prefer public recognition to doing their "homework" and conscientiously working in committees. None of the Irish (or other) politicians who have power ever use the council floor for declaiming on the merits of pending legislation. To some extent, of course, the power-wielders are effective in discouraging council oratory by those who might otherwise be inclined to speak their views on bills being considered in council.

Political Morality

Under English rule the Irish found that government was exclusively self-serving, corrupt, and invariably acted at their expense. This experience bred in them a completely cynical attitude toward government, which anti-Catholic sentiment and the Reform Movement in America perpetuated. Irreconcilably opposed to Protestant society, the Irish were driven into even further social isolation by the political ambitions of reformers whose principles, programs, social style, and activities were as repugnant to the Irish as was their religion.

With such intensely conflicting fundamental social and political values precluding meaningful social interchange, the Irish-Catholic and Protestant-American social structures remained largely uninfluenced by and out of touch with each other over the ensuing decades. This became demonstrably evident in 1947 when the most powerful members (non-Irish)* of the Democratic party's central committee denied Mayor Edward Kelly the customary right to seek reelection by replacing him with Martin Kennelly as the party's nominee. These party leaders recognized

---

* Even among the well-informed there is partial disagreement concerning who the most powerful men in the party were at this time. Most, however, mention Congressman William Dawson and Jacob Arvey.

that the corruption, bribery, and graft so rampant in City Hall during Kelly's administration would no longer be tolerated by an expanding middle class for whom honesty and efficiency in government had become paramount values. An incensed public opinion could no longer be ignored by party officials, and Kennelly, an Irishman with an extremely successful career in business and a prominent civic leader having absolutely no political experience or connection with the party, was nominated for mayor and won the election.

In the years since that event the political values of the Irish politicians have been modified as a result of their growing acceptance of middle-class values, and because they could not otherwise have retained power. Their inclination to give greater favor to the procedural values (honesty, efficiency, and impartiality) insisted on by the reform element and the newspapers was a politically astute move that later was given formal expression in Mayor Daley's statement that "good government is good politics and good politics is good government."

Still, while having accepted such changes because of the persistent demands of the reformers and the new mood of an enlarged and politically concerned middle class, Irish political values continue to stress the problems of the day-to-day operations of government. Irish politicians become extremely annoyed at the unrelenting sniping and harassing of reformers and others who want nothing less than sweeping policy changes legislated without delay. The Irish are convinced that the reformers are hopelessly unaware of the complexities and magnitude of the duties that must be shouldered by those responsible for providing the basic municipal services.

> When you ask reformers how they want to run government they answer, "We don't know." They never have any answers. Just hand Despres [the reform alderman] the ball for one day! What would he do if people like Daley and

Keane came running to him and said, "Why didn't the fire
department answer that call, why wasn't the garbage picked
up, why are the water pumps broken?"

Supposing you do find one policeman stealing something, or a half dozen stealing TV sets. What is this compared with 10,000 police, 5,000 firemen, 15,000 teachers?
When you have to lead that force all they [the reformers]
can do is snap at your heels. It's ridiculous that they can
put up with it—these people have the patience of a Saint.

Although a concern for the quality and direction of civic
life is ever greater among their private interests, the Irish
typically do not incorporate such personal contemplations
into their conception of the most important functions of
government. Their political values, style, and tradition, so
different from the reformers, do not generally permit this.
Instead, they confine their attention to those activities of
government that are most related to the maintenance of
the party—discharging the duties of office effectively
enough to preclude criticism.

. . . the most important thing [in government] is administrative competence. There's only about ten per cent expertise in the most important jobs in administration. There
are certain administrative skills that you learn day in and
day out, and the good administrator precludes the necessity for reform.

I run my office in such a way that you can't criticize my
office if you want to run me for any other office. You could
question my judgment any time you want, but never my
procedures. Anybody can make a mistake in judgment,
but not in procedures.

All this is not to suggest that there are no Irish politicians
who are thoughtfully reflective about the major social
problems of the city. If in the past most of them were engrossed in the problems of the ward and party politics and
patently indifferent (perhaps oblivious) to city-wide issues,
today there are those whose administrative and policy-

making responsibilities compel them to be seriously attentive to the pressing issues of the day and aware of their
wealth of complexity. Issues that stride across metropolitan
and regional areas force themselves upon the attention of
even the indifferent government official.

Despite their having adopted a measure of the reformers' interest in substantive issues, the Irish politicians have
little else in common with them. Even those who believe
that the reformers' role as critics is both necessary and
legitimate have reservations about the reformers' style and
the practicality of the proposals they urge. An Irish alderman, sympathetic to the reformers, said of them:

> . . . they're like a gadfly. They try to get people to move
> faster than is good for themselves and the nation. But they
> do serve a very fine purpose in making the Democratic
> party aware of their needs. They're the only group with a
> social awareness of things.

A view of reformers that is more typical of Irish politicians
was expressed by another alderman who has had considerable personal experience with reformers in the courts and
the council.

> I've been in various positions in cases in court where you
> get an advocate for them, and they can't be reasonable.
> When the law is explained thoroughly and is shown to be
> contrary to their position, they still feel you have sold them
> down the river. When they come before committees, some
> have basically good ideas and you try to bring these ideas
> into a reasonable point of view. But they think you're try-
> ing to undermine their program.
>
> In the council, in Congress, they're devoted to a prin-
> ciple—a damn good principle. You know it can't be ac-
> complished because of the political tenor of the city or
> of your ward. So you try to amend it or talk to them to
> make it palatable, and they think you're trying to under-
> mine their program. This is my observation of reformers

and eggheads. I honestly feel most don't want the social problem they use as their aim or goal to be solved. They'd rather have an issue than a solution to the social problem.

The principle the Irish follow in seeking to settle political problems is that conflicting views should be harmonized by presenting the most generally acceptable proposal. That is, "if you can't accomplish your objective you soften it up and make an approach to it that is satisfactory to the average person. It would be a compromise; something agreeable would come out." The focus of Irish politicians has been on problem-solving and power-maintenance, not problem-creating. Therefore, regardless of how encompassing, genuine, or abiding their own concern about the issues of the day, there are no Irish politicians in Chicago who would sincerely warm to the rhetoric of the reform councilman whose greatest pleasure in city government is

> . . . to have the opportunity to get in direct contact with the problems of the city, and the opportunity to *express* yourself effectively about them and to do something about them. (Emphasis added.)
>
> Politics ought to include planning the city's growth, solving the problems of daily city living, protecting the people in the streets, and using the government to insure a decent living; to use government offices to design the plans to make the city attractive and not oppressive. I think politics, or government, ought to be responsible for helping people live adequately fulfilled lives, to give them an educational opportunity and not to have this denied.*

* Contrast this view with the following comment by an Irish politician: "The feeling [among the Irish] is that everybody takes care of himself. You give food and coal to someone who needs it, but you don't take from somebody else. The Irish don't believe in Aid to Dependent Children. When the Irish came over nobody helped us. We starved, worked, brought ourselves up. . . . When we fought in Ireland we fought the government, that's why the Irish don't look upon social reform as the be-all and end-all."

Irish politicians feel that the reformers' importance is accurately indicated by the numbers they elect to public office.

That particular group [reformers] hasn't any accomplishments. Who'd they ever elect? I don't think they have any effect on the type or character of legislation. You can't control it unless you're in a position to penalize someone for doing something, and they're not. How many have they got in the council? One. They've never had more than one or two.

The political weakness of the reformers is compounded, as the Irish see it, by the visionary character of their goals and the dubious worth of their role as social critics. Thus it is natural that the Irish envisage reformers as publicity-seekers with impracticable aspirations to "revolutionize" society, and as unreasonable because they are generally unamenable to compromise. The Irish consider reformers

. . . difficult people. As a rule they don't appreciate the other person's viewpoint. They are too much the crusader type. They don't realize others can disagree with them and not be personally opposed to them. They associate disagreement with venality, corruption—that is, something against the general good. They either won't compromise or something in their makeup won't allow them to compromise.

Underlying the differences in the views of the Irish and reformers concerning the prospects for political change and the speed at which it can be effected are their contrasting religious beliefs concerning the nature of man. The next comment points up these differences and the importance they have for political action.

Let's take the Calvinist Anglo-Saxon concept of finite government, to achieve perfection in this life through perfect government. The Irish don't give you this premise

straight off. We live to die [the ultimate end is the salvation of the soul]. Thus the Irish are of necessity compro-
misers.[10]

.   .   .   .

Our idea of politics is that you're on the payroll and your
relatives are, too. You do work, but you don't work too
hard. If you're really not hurting anyone or anything
there's no harm done. The classic example is the tree-
trimmers. If you offer them fifty bucks to trim the trees in
your back yard they'll do it. They're not supposed to do it,
but what the hell's wrong with that!? There is a difference
if the battalion chief of the fire department is allowing a
run-down slum to go neglected, or if the police chief al-
lows whorehouses to be run. I think you'll find that these
officials and others wouldn't do favors of that sort, or if
they did they'd do it because they thought you were a nice
guy, not for the money.

For reasons introduced earlier, the Irish have historically
viewed government as a source of power to be used for
individual, rather than social, ends. The political morality
they inherited through the generations has focused on personal needs rather than public interests.

The Irish don't hesitate to ask for a favor or to give one.
With the Irish, it's not taking a gift or a bribe, it's a favor.
The cop doesn't *give*, do something for something, when he
doesn't ticket a car. He doesn't want to give the ticket in
the first place, but he'll forget about giving a ticket as a
favor without expecting it returned. The Irish take their
private morality into public life.

These sociopolitical contrasts are responsible for more
than conflicting views about the possibilities and urgency
of generating social change through governmental action.
They also help to explain the contrasting views of the Irish
and the reformers concerning moral judgments about political decisions and actions, especially regarding whether
or not the "right" decision was made.

Since the decisions and judgments of most Irish politicians are governed by power considerations, they appraise their actions by practicality rather than assessing them according to ethical legitimacy or consistency. Thus, they are very seldom beset by feelings of worry, conflict, or guilt.

> The feeling of guilt, if any, is if there should be a double-cross. [Otherwise,] there should not come into play at all any feeling of guilt. The idealist would say, "guilt"; remorse for having erred, even ethically, over your own or another's action.
>
> In a situation, if something goes wrong, the idealist feels guilt. The realist feels this is human error—someone goofed. we are all subject to frailties, an element of chance is in all situations. Most Irish feel this way. Yes, very few are fraught with a—a—these overwhelming drives that you've got to improve the world, that you've got to straighten the whole thing out by tomorrow. Some have more urgency about them than others, but that is a very different thing. You don't find crusaders among the Irish very often.

Charity

Another aspect of the Irish political style, one that is derived from Ireland's culture as well as from an emphasis the Irish have historically lent to Catholicism, is "charity." That is, it is proper for one to be charitably disposed toward most of the moral and situational shortcomings of others. However, the line is sharply drawn for apostates, heretics, and for marital infidelity, and it is not blindly or universally extended. It generally, though not exclusively, characterizes attitudes, judgments, and actions concerning other Irish.

The Irish do not claim that charitable feelings and gestures toward others are exclusively Irish traits. Rather, it is the nature of their conception of charity and the manner in which it is extended that inform it with "Irishness." The

Irish have a highly tolerant view of human errors and trans-
gressions because of their belief that mortal man, born out
of original sin, is destined to sin, and conventional justice
should therefore be latitudinarian in its judgment of him.
More than that, justice must be tempered with a good deal
of mercy, or charity, for fallible man.

As an integral element of their *modus operandi* in human
relations, their tendency to extend charity (not aid) has
helped the Irish maintain their influence in the party. In
politics as in other avenues of life, the Irish attitude toward
error, incompetence, or infraction of the law is that the
stringency of the formal penalty should be tempered for
humane purposes. Draconian justice neither maintains the
friendliness or support of the errant individual nor recognizes his humanity. In politics, therefore, "you don't humili-
ate a man. That's not done. Wiser heads prevail and he's
given another chance or another job." As the following
observations from several Irish officials make clear, a considerable margin of toleration for human frailties is allowed.

> The Irish are very charitable, much more charitable than
> the others [ethnic groups] by far. You go to some of the
> wards and a poor guy does something—so what? I think an
> Irishman could say, "I might have done the same thing."
> The Irish would be quite a bit more lenient than other
> groups. It's hard for me to fire someone. It's hard for me to
> blow up, but when I do—look out! But one week later I
> take back the guy I fired the week before.

.   .   .   .

> There was a shortage here with regard to the payroll
> when I took over. But it was too late to say anything—it
> wouldn't have helped to begin criticizing. I think the Irish
> are a little more understanding of the frailties of man.

.   .   .   .

> That Smith deal in Stickney—I think the tactics were
> very wrong. He's honest, but he's a self-seeker. I'd have

called them [those accused of stealing the municipal funds] and said, "I know what's going on and I'm not going to stand for it." He [the official who brought charges against other officials] took all the information and then he lowered the boom. . . . Morally, he could have done it more tactfully.

.   .   .   .

Sure, what the hell, give the guy a break, forget it. I must have said that a thousand times. When someone's in trouble, in a jam, it may be financial, legal—assuming the guy prior to that was decent. If he was a rat, to hell with him. Every guy is entitled to a fall, every dog to a bite.

Since the Irish staff so many key administrative positions at various levels of the bureaucracy, their inclination to deal charitably with the needs of others has earned them a reputation as experts in human relations and the gratitude of those whose situation has been eased or improved by them. For example:

When a man is ill in government and without enough time for retirement or health benefit, an efficient man fires him. Yet the Irish administrator says, "What the hell, he has two kids," and keeps him on. He knows this is a risky thing, letting him come in at ten and leave at two. So what happens? He gets a little more work out of the others to make it up.

As one might have anticipated, charity is very much related to one of the major functions of government, as the Irish have traditionally conceived it—to give employment to the "deserving." During the course of an interview, the author could not avoid hearing the following remarks made by an Irish municipal administrator during a telephone conversation with a party official. While discussing a matter of patronage, he argued:

He's deserving! He's got six kids, for God's sake! It would be even a little act of mercy on our part [to give him the job].

In the past far more than in the present, moral laxity among many bureaucratic functionaries and office holders was something less than uncommon. Middle-class standards of honesty and efficiency had not yet gained sufficient sway to make graft, bribery, and minor corrupt practices more, rather than less, hazardous undertakings. Yet enough remains of the traditional Irish attitude toward such questionable ventures, particularly with regard to the comparatively petty ones, to allow the Irish to say of them: "The Irish are forgiving. They don't mind those things; it's a point of business. Making a buck is okay, but don't rob the poor house."

In 1960, when the Chicago police scandal revealed that several policemen had cooperated with criminals in a lucrative burglary ring, the torrent of outraged criticism from the press and a host of civic and business groups did not force a hurried, stammering, or worried retreat by the party or the mayor. Not only was the practice of charity not dispensed with, but the manner in which it was extended was a cool display of *savoir faire*. O'Connor, then the police commissioner, was permitted to submit his resignation for reasons of health and did not become an object of censure by party or government officials. He was granted this opportunity because among the Irish

> . . . there's charity. A winner, there's nothing like success. If you make it good as a commander you get tried on a higher level. If a guy tries it with the regiment and falls down, we wouldn't hit him for it. It's partly our fault for having promoted him to the regiment. We just reduce him to company commander. It's like a series of plateaus—all can't make it to the highest level.

The importance of charity as a political norm among the Irish is also discernible in their self-image. They consider themselves far more charitably disposed toward human shortcomings than Protestant-Republicans, a view that helps maintain the social distance between them and, therefore, the political styles that distinguish them—as this next comment illustrates.

Q.   Is it characteristic of Protestants and of Republicans to be charitable in politics?

A.   Oh, hell no! They want to take the guy out and slaughter him in the streets. The Irish want to give the guy a break every now and then.

One Irish politician who held a high office in government and in the party was denied charity at a critical moment when he was involved in serious legal difficulties that might have terminated his political career. He ended his political future with the Irish by committing what they consider the cardinal sin in politics—he changed parties, an act of shocking disloyalty.

Loyalty

Loyalty, as an intensely personal Irish value, dates from the days when the Irish could turn only to themselves for help and trust when harboring fugitives from English constables, for mutual protection when their secret associations terrorized the countryside, or when small groups of tenant farmers destroyed the property of their landlords. Loyalty to the group—especially to the secret associations—and its cause was absolutely demanded, though at times given with express reluctance by those without personal involvement or unsympathetic to these illicit actions[11] or fearful of retaliatory measures.

Having English authority and Protestantism as the only alternatives to Irish nationalism and Catholicism, loyalty was never an issue for the majority of the Irish. It was a habit. One has only to recall Liam O'Flaherty's, *The Informer*, to sense both the unbearable fear felt by those who broke the code of loyalty and the implacable craving for vengeance by those who had been betrayed.[12] To desert one's friends who were clandestinely and weakly striking

at the powerful English authorities was no less detestable
than forsaking the Church, for in both instances the
"traitor" had deliberately chosen to support Anglo-Saxon
Protestants, the archenemy, at the expense of his persecuted
people and religion.

Thus as the Irish found their way into the urban Democratic parties it was wholly natural, as Potter has shown,
that they carry into these political organizations their basic
political traits.

> Regularity was the first law of the Ribbonmen; regular-
> ity was the cement of Tammany's strength. Catholic Irish-
> men, if ambitious, bucked the regular organization for
> place and preferment but within the organization, and
> when the fight was over, resumed party loyalty. Factional-
> ism was forgivable; deserting to the other party brought
> the severest penalty.[13]

The code of loyalty was just as inviolable in interpersonal
political relationships where its relevance for political success was as important decades ago, when the Irish captured
control of Tammany Hall, as it is today. As Plunkitt, himself, observed:

> The politicians who make a lastin' success in politics
> are the men who are always loyal to their friends, even up
> to the gate of the State prison, if necessary; men who keep
> their promises and never lie. Richard Croker used to say
> that tellin' the truth and stickin' to his friends was the polit-
> ical leader's stock in trade. Nobody ever said anything
> truer, and nobody lived up to it better than Croker. That
> is why he remained leader of Tammany Hall as long as he
> wanted to. Every man in the organization trusted him.
> Sometimes he made mistakes that hurt in campaigns, but
> they were always on the side of servin' his friends.
>
> .   .   .   .
>
> The Irish, above all people in the world, hates a traitor.
> You can't hold them back when a traitor of any kind is in
> sight and, rememberin' old Ireland, they take particular de-

light in doin' up a political traitor. Most of the voters in
my district are Irish or of Irish descent; they've spotted
"The" McManus, and when they get a chance at the polls
next time, they won't do a thing to him.[14]

Irish politicians place great emphasis on loyalty to the
ethnic group, the party, and to each other. However, despite their interest in claiming for themselves as many
offices and as much patronage as their power permits, they
are, nevertheless, usually the first in the party to support
for office that individual, regardless of his ethnic background, who seems to have the best chance to win. Other
ethnic groups are frequently reluctant to adopt this point
of view since they are seeking recognition, and this tends to
blind them to the objective requirements for winning
elections.

If individual Irish politicians on occasion actively con-
test or passively withhold support from a party decision
for personal reasons, they are still far more inclined than
those from other ethnic groups to subordinate their strong
personal interests or resentments after the primary election
so that the party will appear united and its actions concerted and decisive to the electorate. The Irish politicians'
deep sense of loyalty to the party is more than mere organizational commitment; it reflects the long attachment
of the Irish to the party that has been the political home of
working-class Catholics.

Irish politicians also understand loyalty in highly personal terms, especially among themselves, for they first
of all perceive it as related to "people more than to something else." That is, although their symbolic loyalties are
to "religion, party, and adopted country," loyalty is first
of all felt in individualistic and pragmatic terms. Among
Irish politicians a man's word is indeed his bond, and verbal
commitments carry the unequivocal assurance of one's
intention to fulfill his obligations. As one Irish politician

explained it, "politics is a reciprocal thing. If a man can do for me, then I'm for him."

Loyalty, a commanding principle among Chicago's Irish politicians, is above all a symbol of integrity, and disloyalty still carries the invidious connotation of heresy.

> An Irishman wouldn't say, "I'm going to stay in the party but I'll run independent." He wouldn't give up the label he'd worn all his life—*he wouldn't be a turncoat.**
>
> If something happened to me, dumped [refused renomination] for some reason, I'd stay in the party, but in the next election I'd have my petition circulated for office. (Emphasis added.)

Loyalty is sustained even today by the inherited memories of the religious and political struggles the Irish waged with Britain and by personal familiarity with religious and social discrimination in the United States. In the course of mentioning the strong similarities between the Democratic and Republican political views of urban government, an Irish politician nevertheless argued for party loyalty in terms of the age-old religious conflict, stating:

> I have no difficulty over principles at the local level; both parties are pretty much the same. But I can never join the Republican organization. It's always been my understanding that you don't change. I respect the Republican who won't change his party more than the one who does. "Taking the soup" [changing parties]—it goes back to the religious aspects and the rest, to the British, joining the other side.**

---

* According to an Irish alderman, "_____ was the great hope of all the Irish at one time, but he pulled up lame because he didn't have a sense of loyalty to the organization that was felt necessary."

** Among Irish politicians in Chicago the term "fallen away" has a political as well as religious connotation. For example, if one Irish politician said to another at ward headquarters, "Say, I haven't seen

It is partly in terms of their strong feelings about loyalty that the Irish distinguish other ethnic politicians from themselves. An eminently successful veteran Irish politician alluded to this, saying:

> One thing about the Irish, they're frank. If we've committed ourselves, given our word, you know just where we stand. If they don't like you they'll tell you. So many other groups dance from here to there—they want to be with a winner. There's an old political philosophy, "I'd rather lose with a somebody than win with a nothing."[15]
> Even when he goes down to a loss, an Irishman is proud. He feels "at least we showed them." So many other nationality groups can be herded. They're real great if they're in front, but when they're losing—the Italians and Poles— they just don't want to fight back.

Another politician derisively described one of the groups in the Democratic party, by saying, "the _____ are either at your feet or your throat—they have all the characteristics of a dog except loyalty."

A telling, and perhaps classic, example of the emphasis the Irish give to political loyalty is found in an incident that occurred not too many years ago about which Irish politicians still speak with a profound sense of shock. A non-Irish official sought (without adequate grounds, as it turned out) legally to jeopardize the career of another official who shared his national ancestry. The latter's father had been quite influential in assisting the first official in launching his political career.

> What was staggering to the Irish was the betrayal of [X] by [Y] who was set up in politics by [X's] father. Then [Y] turned around and stabbed the son of a man who befriended him. Time and again the comment was heard

---

Delehanty lately," and his companion replied, "Oh, he's fallen away," the latter would mean that Delehanty became a Republican.

[among the Irish], "How!?" The Irish couldn't understand, but the _____ [nationality group] could. Their attitude was, "a guy's got to get ahead."

The thing _____ did—he picked on his own kind! . . . You don't hurt your own if you can avoid it. To me it was almost—I don't know how to describe it! I didn't like it. You might have an intra-party fight among the Irish, but *nothing* like that.

On occasion individual Irish politicians are faced with the difficult choice of supporting either a close personal friend or the party's nominee whom he is challenging in the primary. Despite the fact that most of them support the party at the primary election, the Irish greatly esteem the individual who "stands up," whose loyalty to a friend takes precedence over party obligation.

Such an incident occurred when the late John Duffy (then committeeman of the Nineteenth Ward Regular Democratic Organization) supported Mayor Martin Kennelly in the Democratic primary of 1955, despite the party's having agreed upon Richard Daley as its nominee for mayor. Duffy's alignment with Kennelly was based upon his close ties with Kennelly and with Thomas Nash, Duffy's predecessor as committeeman, who had been a long-time friend of Kennelly. Recognizing this, Irish ward committeemen and Daley felt no animosity toward Duffy. In fact, Daley is reputed to have said, "If I were on the other [Duffy's] side I would bolt." In spite of his opposition during the primary, Duffy (a political power in his own right, and later president of Cook County Board of Commissioners) and Daley worked very closely and cooperatively with each other in party affairs after the election, for Duffy's action in this situation had in no way violated the code of loyalty. Irish standards permit certain personal loyalties to supersede loyalty normally due the party.

The bond of loyalty remains firm even in instances when highly independent Irish politicians run against the party in primary elections. Judge Michael L. Igoe, for example, commanded sufficient respect to have been rewarded with an appointment to the federal bench rather than having been cast out of the party for having run against its candidate for governor in the 1932 primary election. Another Irish politician who remained in the party's favor after having challenged it in the primary is Judge Thomas J. Courtney, who ran against Mayor Kelly in 1939. The most recent example of an Irish politician who unsuccessfully contested the party (for the nomination as State's Attorney in 1952) yet who did not lose favor in the party, is Judge John J. Boyle, whose appointment as Chief Judge of the Circuit Court of Cook County was to some extent guided by the preferences of Mayor Daley.

The fuller significance of political loyalty deals with political success. However important individual political achievements may be, at times they are entirely contingent upon considerations of personal loyalty that may oblige the Irish politician to take actions that will cost him his office in government, and perhaps his position in the party as well. As an Irish municipal official observed:

> The only criterion of success in politics is success. Right? Not with the Irish. There are all sorts of guys out of office who did the right thing in the right way or the wrong thing the right way. You must be loyal to your friends and enemies. I've heard the saying that "you've got to punish your enemies or your friends will probably wonder if you'll be loyal to them." Sometimes you've got to "stand up" even if it means going down.*

* An Irish politician discussing Duffy's decision to support Kennelly, said: "Why did Duffy back Kennelly instead of Daley when he knew the party suffered with Kennelly and that Daley was needed to restore the party's strength? There's always such things as obliga-

The style through which personal political loyalties are expressed has an importance of its own; action is taken quietly, without ceremony, fanfare, or effusiveness, especially by those holding higher positions or with aspirations to reach higher levels. For that matter, loyalty to others is best exemplified when one takes the appropriate action without being called upon to do so.

> You've got to be a man of your word, trustworthy. You can't be petty or cheap. If I say, "I'll put your brother on the payroll," your brother must be put on the payroll. That's common courtesy. Putting it into eloquence that transcends description, you put him on the payroll before you've been asked. Then, decline the thanks of the person who asked you—"it's nothing." Thanks aren't necessary.

Power-seeking

People are attracted to politics for many reasons. Some enjoy its excitement and color; others find an appeal in the issues and the candidates' personalities; for certain persons politics affords an escape from the monotony of their daily routine; still others are attracted to party meetings and campaigns by the opportunity to make new acquaintances; and there are those who find vicarious satisfaction as hangers-on—the sycophants who delight in basking in the glory of the politicians. But for those for whom politics is a full-

---

tions which, if turned down, your own people would run away. The only thing you have in politics is your word—break your word and you're dead. The most successful politician is the politician who kept his word, even at the expense of his own status—though he may come back. Had Duffy forsaken them, his own people would say he didn't 'stand up' under pressure."

"This is the Irishman's forte. Once given, if he breaks his word the others will go out of their way to undermine him. If he goes down, he goes down, but he goes down rather than take the easy way out and go with the one who wins."

time vocation—a business—the chief incentives are money,
power, and status, and it is scarcely contestable that each
has a strong appeal for all who regard politics as a career.
For the Irish, however, the acquisition of power has been
and continues to be the most compelling of these inducements.

The motives that have most attracted the Irish into politics are:

> . . . probably a compromise between power and glory.
> Money enters into it somewhat, but I don't think you can
> explain it on the basis of money, at least not over a length
> of time. It would have to consistently be explained in
> terms of power and glory. The idea appeals to the average
> Irishman. That is, "If I'm not in power, what can I do?"
> As the Irish analyze it, power is dominant and glory is
> second. I say "power" without assessing the motives for
> it—whether it's power for its own sake or power to be used
> for the people. The Irish tried to present a type of govern-
> ment that makes it possible for them to stay in power.

Other ethnic groups in the party, unlike the Irish, are
less interested in power than in social mobility and mone-
tary gain. It is the experience of Irish politicians that these
other ethnic groups ". . . fritter away their power. Most are
bought off. It seems that they go into politics for money."
It certainly is clear that the nature of the Irish interest in
power would never permit an Irish politician to act as Judge
_____ did, giving up "the political leadership of the Poles
for the position of Federal District Judge. . . . Daley, when
he was County Clerk, would never have done anything like
that."

In this and earlier chapters it is clear how difficult it has
been for the Irish to yield to the attractions of upward social mobility as a result of religio-class barriers. However,
the Irish in politics have been far more subject to these

constraints than have the Irish in other occupations. The Irish politicians have held the most exemplary occupational roles among the Irish, for whom an outward expression of material affluence and social and occupational mobility smacked of the proscribed Protestant style of life. Consequently, the financial and status achievements that the Irish, especially the Irish politicians, achieved could be enjoyed and expressed only in terms of the ethnic norms which dictated that they be savored inconspicuously. This conservative social style obtained with full force for any Irishman with political ambitions, but left him the highly Irish-approved goal of *power* to pursue as ambitiously as he was inclined. In this sense there is an interesting parallel between the Irish politician and the Irish priest.

With a tradition that gave them a pervading desire for power, the reason why so many Irishmen entered city politics in America now becomes clearer. Apart from whatever other inducements led them into government as functionaries, administrators, or elective officials, power has for centuries had an inordinate appeal to the Irish as their most highly approved secular value.

> The Irish inherited the desire of political control so they could have something to say about things, about the way they went. It's a natural, inherent characteristic to want to be in control.
>
> The Irish don't want money; they want power. They don't spend their time throwing thunderbolts—that's not dignified. They have a hoard in the basement and they don't relinquish it. With _____ and _____ [non-Irish politicians], power can be bought like kilowatts. By and large they're right, but can't you imagine them going to see Daley and asking him to exchange some of his power for money!

Their absorption in power considerations and their differences in social class and style constitute the basis for their still strongly critical views of those who prefer the political satisfactions of status and money.* More importantly, their power-orientation helps explain why the Irish have remained in politics over time and have been so successful in dealing with their competitors in the party.

The Irish found the Democratic party a congenial and convenient avenue to power which, because it had few religious or class qualifications, allowed them to identify with it almost completely. Once involved in the party and government, the Irish, having far stronger power and lesser status interests in politics than other ethnic groups, were in a strategic position to play off one group against the other. Furthermore, the intra-party animosities and jealousies of the other ethnic groups helped the Irish assume the role of party mediators—those who, in their established position of power, could best effect compromises acceptable to the others.** A Park District official described this role of the Irish:

* The other ethnic groups in the Democratic party have sought political representation far more for the advantages of status, social mobility, and economic opportunity, rather than for the gratifications that power brings. With vastly different backgrounds, they had no reason—as had the Irish—to fuse politics with their ethnic cultures. For these groups, politics has been an acculturating influence, whereas for the Irish it has been an ethnic bond. Even among the affluent Irish in the Nineteenth Ward, those who are in ward politics are "in it for the sheer love of the game, not for any benefit."

Those Irish politicians who, like Edward J. Flynn (who for many years was the boss of the Democratic party in the Bronx), have sought higher positions to gratify status ambitions have broken away from their social moorings somewhat sooner than others.

** According to an Irish alderman, "The Irish have a greater ability to compromise than other groups. I've seen other promising politicians in other ethnic groups who have a blind spot regarding compromise. They are not as skillful as I was led to believe they were."

The Irish are what you might call a compromise. Here, take the Polish. Very few Polish will vote for a Lithuanian, and vice versa. Very few Italians will vote for a Pole, and Poles for an Italian. So the Irish are sort of a compromise of the whole conglomeration and seem to be able to pacify all nationalities. It's natural intuition, I guess—I know it is with me.

Apropos of their skill in maneuvering the other groups so adroitly, Congressman William Dawson (Committeeman of the Second Ward and for over two decades the powerful boss of Chicago's Negro political organization) is reputed to have remarked with admiration to an Irish politician, "You Irish don't realize you're a minority group."

It is true, of course, that there have been Irish politicians who have profited immensely from administrative and elective positions. For the most part, the graft they (and others) enjoyed belongs to yesteryear, when contractors and utility and traction companies were building the physical plant of the city. In those days they were shockingly generous and blatant in buying votes in the city council, or in supplying campaign funds to assure themselves of candidates whose votes they could control. It is also true, however, that those Irish politicians who subordinated the power motive to their taste for ostentatious high living, such as Alderman John (Bathhouse) Coughlin, were not (or did not remain) influential officeholders or power-wielders in the party. For example, control of the First Ward, which he represented for many years, passed into the hands of Mike (Hinky-Dink) Kenna, a quiet, unassuming man, who managed the affairs of the ward organization in a businesslike manner on a year-round basis.* Coughlin's penchant for

* ". . . Kenna was the glummest little man in the entire ward organization. Coughlin was the accomplished backslapper; Kenna cared little for gay companionship and was aloof almost to the point of snobbery. Coughlin laughed at everyone's jokes, asserting his

gaudy clothing, bombastic speeches, outings at the race
track, acquisition of a race horse, and extravagant mode of
travel were neither in keeping with Irish tastes nor permitted him time for the effective supervision of the business
of the ward organization.

Those Irish politicians who struck the author as most
reticent, tough, and decisive were said to be either the most
influential Irish in the party or individuals who seemed to
have a promising future. These men were also more given
than others to discuss political power, as well as to reveal a
fascination with the intricacies and subtleties of power
struggles in the party from which they derived considerable satisfaction.* Speaking about an important power play
with which he was familiar, one Irish politician mused:

> God knows I'm not in politics for the money. The main
> thing I enjoy is the problem-solving point—there's such
> joy in that. This gave me great satisfaction recently and I
> laughed till I could hardly stand. The cause was a major
> victory solved in Chicago [party politics]. When I think of
> those morons who will go to their grave never understand-

---

friendship for every man, and sought votes in his bathhouse precinct
by knocking on doors and personally extolling the multifold attributes of the party candidates; Kenna spoke sparingly, rarely
smiled, counted only a picked few as his friends, and organized the
saloon hangers-on as a corps of precinct captains to make door-to-
door calls and offer promises of free beer and lunch. Coughlin was
all sound and fury; Kenna was silence and action." Wendt and Kogan, *op. cit.*, pp. 75-6.

* A non-Irish politician said of the Irish that "there's a saying
that the Irish [politicians] are sentimental. That stuff is nonsense.
They're cold-blooded as hell." This person had been an ineffective
ward committeeman who lost his position. Other non-Irish politicians interviewed who were dubious about Irish "sentimentality" had
either chosen the wrong faction in a power fight among Irish factions or had themselves lost out to the Irish. Irish politicians most
respected those, Irish and non-Irish, who are tough, aggressive—and
skillful— in wielding power.

ing how it happened! I didn't get two cents richer, and certainly in my prestige and power there's no difference in my quota. It was the sheer delight of seeing these people—they were at ground zero when the bomb went off. This thing had major cataclysmic reverberations. It was the sheer delight in seeing those no-good bastards go up in smoke.

The Irish fascination with power,* including their knowledgeable aggressiveness and consummate skill in wielding it, is not confined to politics. Competitiveness and power plays are an ingrained aspect of the Irish way of life and partake of none of the stigma with which power-orientation is branded by other elements in this society. The remarks below suggest the extent to which power interests characterize Irish social behavior.

[An interest in power] is very distinctively a part of Irish culture. Life is a challenge and a curiosity piece. In a crowd of Irish it's always one-upmanship. It's not a personal thing, but in a friendly sort of way you play the game—with no malice. You get a bang out of seeing some mope play a fast one. When he thinks he has it made, suddenly you come in and say—"What are you doing there!"

Power, through its institutionalization, display, and exercise in the Church, as well as its having been constantly used to serve the interests of the English landlords and government, became as integral a part of Irish culture as did

* An acquaintance of the author related the following tale. While in the Army during World War II he had been assigned to a clerical position where he worked with an Irishman. One day they were lolling under a tree where, from a distance, they watched a parade of all the soldiers stationed at the camp. The Irishman said quietly, "Isn't that a great sight?" and his companion sarcastically replied, "Oh, sure, it really is a striking spectacle and makes a man feel very patriotic." The Irishman remonstrated, "No, I really mean it—isn't that an impressive parade!" When his companion answered, "I don't understand what you mean," the Irishman said, "Who do you think put them out there [wrote the order]?"

economic destitution and religious animosity. The drama, harshness, symbols, and omnipresence of power so penetrated the lives of the Irish that their engrossment with it was a habit certainly not to be discarded or forgotten as immigrants in a new Protestant culture.

The Irish are not apt to shrink from an opportunity to gain power. Nor, on the other hand, do they hold or use it rigidly as martinets unaccustomed to having power who are manifestly uncertain and ill at ease as its possessors.* The Irish, if they can be exceedingly and unflinchingly tough, are equally known for exercising power confidently, firmly, and with a practical appreciation of restraint. The Irish attitude toward the exercise of power is that "You don't crack a whip because you may be the horse again some day. There have been all sorts of Irish bosses, but an Irish tyrant is unheard of."

The Irish sense of restraint and anticipation is also important in their negotiations with so many claimants for power in the party.

> The Irish use the expression, "You're too big for petty vengeances." You humiliate your enemy with kindness rather than by exacting retribution, and you're a bigger man for it—you get grace for it.

Because they were both religiously and secularly deprived of opportunities to give serious consideration to becoming genuinely interested in the variety of ends to which governmental power could be directed, politics served the essential function of reaffirming the ethnic identity of Irish politicians. Until their social structure broke out of its cul-de-sac, power would remain the preeminent goal of Irish politicians. It is for this reason that Moynihan has written:

> . . . the Irish did not know what to do with power once they got it. . . . They never thought of politics as an instrument

* See Appendix C.

of social change—their kind of politics involved the processes of a society that was not changing.[16]

THE BOND OF *Irish* CATHOLICISM

The values people treasure most highly are the prisms through which they view, differentiate, and deal with their social universe. Consequently, these values are the principal means by which they acquire their sense of social identity, however well or inadequately developed it may be.

The most authoritative value of the Irish, the one that has been most responsible for the ethnic identity they realized, has been their very special sense of Catholicism—*Irish* Catholicism. This has been, and continues to be, the critical component of Irish identity and solidarity, to the extent that each has significance today. Having lost most of their social base of support as their neighborhoods and parishes dwindled or disappeared in the course of the Irish dispersion throughout Chicago and into the suburbs, *Irish* Catholicism has increasingly become the one remaining element enabling the Irish to retain their now marginal and ever diminishing ethnic distinctiveness. Its great and continuing hold on the Irish still springs mainly from the rancor contained in the memories and experiences stemming from the Catholic-Protestant religious cleavage. Refusing or unable to disengage themselves from the tenacious grip of history, some Irish still feel that "if the English joined the Church, the Irish would leave it."

Irish politicians probably are somewhat more acutely aware of their special kind of Catholicity than are the Irish who are not in politics. Unlike the latter, they have been forced to contend daily with a variety of other ethnic groups to whom they have yielded power that once was theirs. Continually faced with competitors for power within the party, as well as from without, Irish politicians have not had as great an opportunity as other Irish in our times to overlook the social differences of others which heighten their own sense of identity. In addition, Irish politicians vividly remember their long history of persecution and discrimination in this country and carefully point out that "the Czechs and Poles never had the sting of persecution. They were discriminated against as 'hunkies,' and not as Catholics, and not [discriminated against as Catholics] in the old country."

With well over a century behind them since the first large groups of Irish immigrants came to the United States, today's Irish politicians still have a strong sense of identity and solidarity, which is kept viable by the different religious attitudes of other Catholics. An Irish committeeman pointed up these differences between the Irish and the other Catholics, saying:

> If you ask an Irishman what he feels a good Catholic is, he'll say there is a feeling of two parts about the Church—good faith and he doesn't run around with other women. If you ask an Italian, or most Latins, he'll say something that's kind. He might be a lot more right than the Irish. We're a lot more puritanical than the Italians.

As concerns the first stricture, an Irishman could fall into no greater disrepute among other Irish than to apostatize or convert, and this holds with at least equal, and probably greater, force for Irish politicians. Each of them is to some degree dependent upon the good will and acceptance of the other Irish politicians in the party who would ostracize any Irishman who intentionally left the Church. That such a politician would also lose his power is certain. Although not necessarily exemplars of the faith, all Irish politicians interviewed regularly attended Sunday Mass and about twenty-five per cent indicated that they also attended Church on holy days of obligation.

The other human shortcoming the Irish condemn as an unspeakable sin is marital infidelity, and all Irish politicians are fully cognizant of its general significance and how it can jeopardize a political career. As one of them noted:

> I think the moral standard demanded by the people at the head of the party, from a sex standpoint, is very high. I know people passed up for advance, though they would have done a good job, because they caroused around with the other sex.[17]

Another made the same point in the course of comparing the lenient attitude the Irish have toward other human failings, remarking that

> [the Irish] attitude on marriage is a big factor. If a man comes home drunk or is caught with his hand in the till, they say "poor fellow." But just let him run around with women—it's unforgivable! The Sixth Commandment is unforgivable [sic]—the rest, "Ah, the Lord forgives." It's okay if he comes home drunk, swears, but not running around with women.

This caveat even affects the non-Irish who associate closely with the Irish in important political matters. An instance of this occurred when a man upon whom Mayor Daley has frequently relied for advice sent his secretary in a separate taxi to a meeting with high-level Irish politicians that they both attended. He took this action expressly to avoid raising the faintest trace of suspicion among the Irish politicians attending the meeting. From the Irish point of view, "You can get away with a lot of things in politics if you maintain fidelity to your family. It's not so true of other nationalities."

The nature of their commitment to Catholicism, as well as their manner of affirming it, leads Irish politicians to distinguish other Catholics in terms of criteria that are inapplicable to themselves. That is, they visualize these other groups both as *Catholics* with religious attitudes and practices different from their own and as *ethnic groups* distinguished by unique customs. By way of contrast, Irish politicians feel certain that the Irish in general are "better" Catholics than members of other nationalities, and in this respect are especially critical of Italians who go to Church just "three times in their lives—when they're baptized, married, and when they die." In addition, it is the conviction of Irish politicians that the scope and intensity of the religious concern of other ethnic groups is far less than it ought to be.

> With other groups of Catholics only women are in church. Among the Irish the men are as active and have as much deep-seated religion and faith, and this makes a completely different atmosphere in the home and community. The best explanation I can give [for other Catholics] is that the attendance of religious services is predominantly by women. This is not true of the Irish.

The Irish are further differentiated from other ethnic Catholics by the contrasting ways in which they define their identities. Since religion has been the most vital part, and is today really the only remaining component, of their identity, Irish politicians view other Catholics as having divided loyalties. That is, the latter interpret and modify religious doctrine through their cultural values. For the Irish, on the other hand, Catholicism *is* their culture. For example,

> . . . the Polish Catholic has greater loyalty to being a Pole than the Irish do to being Irish. The Irish are more Irish Catholics, and a Pole is more a Pole. . . . If the Church gave out a ruling that every Irishman should take a bath every hour, the Irish would. The Italian wouldn't.

This difference has introduced another dimension in terms of which Irish politicians distinguish themselves from other Catholics. Irish Catholicism is identical with a staunch, Church-oriented outlook and commitment which is at the core of Irish identity. Therefore, the Irish have taken a deprecating view of the nature of the other ethnic groups' commitment to the Church. Their relationship to the Church, as an Irish city official pointed out, is more independent than is the Irish. He said:

> The Church holds us together. There's a common interest when you're thinking about something and the Church comes up—we all understand it the same way. The Irish take the Church a lot more seriously [than the others]. It's not what the Church can do for them. The Poles and Italians are serious, all right, but they're more serious in terms of what they want out of the Church.

The independence of these other groups from the Church is attributable to the fact that they derive little, if any, of their identity or solidarity from their association with Catholicism. Thus, where anticlerical sentiments are harbored, as with the Italians, there is a decided tendency to deal with the Church, its officials, and dicta as though one had "joined" the Church rather than as though one were a part of it. An Irish priest offered this analysis of their relationship:

> There's a kind of Italian piety that's typical of the Italians. The Italians are thought of as anti-clerical and the Irish as the typical organization men of the Church. Italians are funny because they can be very devout and intent Catholics, but they have a different relationship to priests. They don't support the priests financially. Many more are suspicious of priests. They look upon the priest as causing a lot of trouble and *would rather deal directly with God*. (Emphasis added.)

Another of the variations in ethnic attitudes toward priests also suggests the extent to which the Church itself acts as a unifying influence for the social identities of ethnic Catholics. The greater significance of this relationship for the Irish than for other Catholics has found its way into an anecdote about an Irishman, an Italian, and a Pole, which was told the author by an Irish priest.

> A priest is working in the garden in front of the rectory and three men walk by. The first one says, "Let me do that for you Father." The second says, "This is how you do it, Father." The third man walks by and pretends not to see the priest. What is the national ancestry of each of the men?*

One further distinction between the Irish and other Catholics is that the Church has been and continues to be the only "social" organization of any significance in which the Irish have (and *feel* they have) membership as Irish. Other ethnics frequently are members of ethnic social organizations that further the retention of their ethnic identity. The Irish, however, typically belong to no Irish social organizations that are not associated with the Church. Consequently, the Church is their one social bond.

> The religious tie has a lot to do with it [maintaining Irish solidarity]. I, for one, and so many I associate with socially, belong to no Irish society of any kind. Whether in industry, business, or politics, the only tie we have is the Church. It ties us together more than anything else. The Irish Fellowship Club meets together and eats once a year—on St. Patrick's Day. Those who do join [Irish] social groups are usually greenhorns or who are just one generation away.

The linguistic and cultural differences of the other ethnic politicians (which are far less quickly and easily lost than were the Irish brogue and customs, even over the same

* The answer is: Irish, Polish, and Italian.

period of time) constantly remind the Irish politicians of the significant differences that remain between them and their ethnic competition.

> When the Irish go back to their old customs they go to Hanley's [tavern] where they speak English. But when the Pole goes back [to the old customs] he speaks Polish and divorces himself from the English language and immediately drops the gate of culture. Two more generations when he goes back to a Polish club he will then have the same mobility as the Irish, and will find that peculiar thing, that we're all altar boys—a common ethic of tradition.*

The diverse social attachments of the other ethnic Catholics also help to differentiate them from the Irish in political matters. The Poles, Italians, and others are members of ethnic social organizations that occasionally press elected officials with various kinds of political demands. The Irish, however, have traditionally been represented by the Church and the ward organization rather than by ethnic associations, and have been well entrenched in the party and government. As a result, they have not approached government or party officials for favors or assistance on the basis of their ethnicity. These differences in social ties incline the Irish to look upon the other ethnics as very clannish in political affairs.

---

* The "common ethic of tradition"—"that we're all altar boys"— is elaborated upon on p. 200. The Irish tend to regard those other ethnics who have most assimilated and are as serious about politics as themselves as most like Irish politicians. "There are a number of people who have the same 'ethic' the Irish have. For example, you could call him O'Rourke and his name is R_____, Dwyer and D_____, Casey and C_____," all of whom are Polish politicians.

Of another Polish politician it was said that "[he] is an exception, an outstanding individual. He said [in 1960] of the slate, 'never mind one of ours [Adamowski, the Republican candidate for State's Attorney], we're Democrats and we're supporting Ward.' His closest friends are Irish—*he's more assimilated.*" (Emphasis added.)

The Irish don't say, "I'm sent from the Hibernians." They say, "I'm from such and such a ward." The others come from ethnic organizations. The Irish don't do it that way. They're very individualistic.

Politics in Chicago's Democratic party has been, and largely remains, a struggle among ethnic groups for power, and this has redounded to the advantage of the Irish. That is, while the Irish have had to award committeemanships to the other ethnic groups in the wards of their densest population, they have been comparatively free from such pressures in wards with ethnic diversity or in those whose residents were assimilated. Thus, as a result of the Irish having dispersed through most parts of the city, Irish politicians could easily support other Irish for the office of committeeman in these wards. Once in control of them, it is virtually impossible to unseat the Irish committeemen whose patronage resources made their positions almost impregnable. Furthermore, it is more likely than not that the Irish, with Anglicized names and no linguistic differences, have been more acceptable to the constituents of heterogeneous or assimilated wards than other ethnics have been.

The Parochial School Ethos and System of Authority

Until recent years, when its stringent system of authority and discipline began to yield to the centrifugal forces of assimilation,* the parochial school system was by far the

---

* "Parochial school was good preparation for life, not only for politics. Discipline stands you in good stead for the years ahead. They don't conduct them like they used to when we were going to school. God Almighty!—if we stepped out of line we got our knuckles rapped by the nuns, and we didn't tell our parents when we got home or we'd get another belt! They very definitely lack cooperation from the parents today. The parents want to go back and rap the teacher or the nun.

I say that the reason parochial schools were successful was be-most important formal influence during the formative years of its students. As an educational monolith existing apart from the changes affecting the larger society, the parochial school claimed a remarkable degree of consensus ·with regard to the educational, social, and religious values it represented. Essentially under the control of Irish priests, it was one of the keystones in the Irish social structure—the importance of which for Irish politicians is attested below:

> The same social order has produced the politicians and the clergy. . . . We've staffed the clerical echelons, and a good Irish politician is a semi-monastic man, anyway. All Irish are proud of a man who doesn't drink—we're puritanical. *The clergy and politics got the best we produced.*[18] (Emphasis added.)

Some further consideration of the effects of this educational system is pertinent for the reason that, as one politician remarked, the parochial school experience is responsible for "keeping the Irish [politicians] together."

Because of the Church's defensive position for most of its history, the parochial school became primarily a system of education whose first duty was to maintain the faith of its communicants, a task that could be best achieved by commanding their unqualified respect for its authority. Its teachers—the priests, nuns, and brothers—were the authority figures of the Church purposely chosen to represent and serve its interests. Thus, this system of education was necessarily one that could neither encourage nor permit serious dissent over educational questions or about the authority of the teachers, for this would have been the

---

cause of the cooperation between the parent and the school, and it's sorely lacking today. My wife goes up to the parochial school one day a week—there are 2300 kids at _____ Church and they ask the mothers to help out, to keep order among the kids. Why those kids have no more respect for us than the man in the moon. They openly defy you." (From an interview with an Irish alderman.)

equivalent of disrespect for and a weakening of the authority of the Church. The importance, legitimacy, and distribution of authority were immediately made clear to all students, an interest of sufficient importance to the Church that the practice has continued into the present. As Fichter has written of the parochial school in recent times, "the lines of authority are explained [to third grade students] through the Fourth Commandment, from pupil to teacher to Principal to Pastor to Bishop to Pope to God."[19]

A tightly controlled educational system that justifies its directives and emphases by relying upon remote and indisputable authorities from whom its power has been delegated focuses the attention of those to whom it ministers on its own power centers. Its own steady, strong, and omnipresent authority, therefore, can hardly help but become a focal point for those most sensitized to the nature and uses of the power it wields. The significance of the relationship is best illustrated through the observations of a politician who went to parochial school. His perceptive recollections merit being quoted at length to avoid omitting the nuances that would be lost in a paraphrased account. In response to a question dealing with the basic reasons for the continuing solidarity of the Irish politicians, this official said:

> Maybe you can say we're all altar boys. . . . A guy in the Nineteenth or Thirty-Eighth Ward, if I discuss religion with them we'd be similar. Our morality—cutting out the religious end—when you do this and that [in politics], would be goddamn near the same. What's right and wrong. Ask any two of us the same questions involving moral or ethical teaching regarding judgment [political] decisions and I'd bet we'd run almost one hundred per cent identical even though we hadn't met each other.
>
> The common bond expresses itself in inane and crazy ways. A guy looked at me in a law office the other day and

said, "Did you go to _____ University? Well, so did I."
We kind of—click!

The parochial schools are responsible. . . . They're responsible for the oneness of the ethic. They have stricter
discipline. If this kind of discipline was used in the public
schools there'd be ten thousand law suits. At _____,
brother, you'd better get with it—there's no going to see Mr.
Willis. You'll get belted up and down the corridor. There's
none of this sit-in protest bit!

There is usually a title, the Prefect of Discipline. He'll
say, "Now somebody here is in some kind of disagreement
with me and it's spread to everyone. Since I don't know who
started it and won't be able to find out, I'll read every
third name." You get jugged [detained] for one month. You
get home at 5:00 p.m. or 6:00 p.m. Or, he may say, "every
tenth one is suspended."

The parochial school system so thoroughly gained Irish
acceptance of its authority and educational values that a
permissive educational system in which academic argu-
mentation is the norm appears as a baffling contrast, as the
next account makes evident.

My first experience with non-Catholic education was in
graduate school at _____ University. One day there were
six of us talking together—from Marquette, Georgetown,
Holy Cross, two from Notre Dame, and one from Loyola.
After the third week we were sitting around one day
watching the stuff that was going on in the class rooms.
What the hell is this!? I've had sixteen years of education
in Catholic schools and when I graduated the same administration was there. It was the administration against us and
us against them. I didn't know what was going on here. The
difference was staggering—you're stunned!*

* The following is from an interview with an Irish graduate stu-
dent who discussed his parochial school experiences in Cleveland,
Ohio.
"The students were united against the system and when there

You can go through the roster of [Irish] city officials and
they're all from De La Salle. If they did in public high
school what they did there you'd have a federal committee
investigating the whole system. You shape up or get out
[of parochial school]. I think this educational background
after a while instills self-discipline in you if you can sur-
vive, and it's a real question of survival.*

Politics, too, is a "real question of survival." However,
Irish politicians have had considerable preparation for it.
Indeed, most of their history has been a series of experiences with systems of authority that provided them with
vivid illustrations and instructive encounters with the uses
of power. Their political style reflected their reactions to
these experiences, but in recent years it has been modified
by the irresistible force of the economic and social changes
that have destroyed Chicago's insularity and its variegated
ethnic character by transforming it into a metropolis with
a middle-class base and ethos. These same forces are also
chiefly responsible for attracting the Irish to the many occupations they created and for edging the Irish away from
government and party positions toward which, in the past,
they naturally gravitated and claimed almost as a matter
of prerogative.

---

was an opening they'd rush toward it. And then, of course, the
teachers would move. If you ever got punished at school you never
complained when you got home cause then you'd get it again from
your parents."

* The importance of Catholic education as a unifying influence
for Irish politicians was expressed somewhat differently by an official
with the city government, who said: "There's a difference between
_____ and myself. He's fourth generation Irish and I'm third. He
went out into society to get an education, and I stayed in Chicago.
But look at the people he went to school with—the sons of Irish politicians, just like mine, except that my classmates were the sons of
judges and policemen from Chicago. . . . The system's the same,
whether it's Loyola, Fordham, Georgetown, Notre Dame, etc."

Conclusion 7

Chicago's Irish politicians are not yet on the verge of vanishing from the political scene, although their future in politics is not encouraging. This becomes more evident in the "successors" they have brought into government and the party, the "new" Irish, who are the last of the line as well as a different political type. The "new" Irish politicians are typically college graduates, usually with degrees in law or engineering, and some have married women from other ethnic backgrounds. For the most part, they live in middle-class neighborhoods where ethnic differences are more remembered than discernible, and they often socialize with acquaintances of different ethnic ancestries and religious faiths. As a result, their children are growing up with scarcely any ethnic identity, and what little they may retain is due more to their attendance of parochial schools than to family influence.

Among the small but growing number whose expertise qualifies them for their positions in government, the "new" Irish politicians in some cases have no meaningful relation-

203

ship to the party. One of them, a bureaucrat in the municipal government commented on this, saying, "I was never a precinct captain and don't even know who the captain in my precinct is." Nevertheless, he, like the other younger Irish politicians, is a product of the Irish family-based sponsorship system, which, though it still influences official selection from the eligible civil service candidates, is gradually losing its function. The growing need for skilled personnel in responsible administrative positions curtails the scope of the patronage system. As one of the younger Irish politicians explained it:

> Many departments have people without sponsors today. What the hell are you going to do!? You've got to have people who can audit and you can't get them out of the precincts. You can train almost anyone for clerical jobs, but they've got to be educated and have ability if they want jobs in administration.

At lesser levels, which today attract fewer Irish than ever before, technology has eliminated jobs that were once essential to the patronage system; elevators in city hall (but not on the county's side of the building) are automated, and new machines are now used to maintain accounts of tax receipts, traffic violations, and other records. The wellsprings of patronage are drying up at the upper levels, too, where appointments are no longer so easily come by through a sponsor's intercession because of the dictates of prudence and objective necessity. The growth of professionalization, the inevitable consequence of the far greater complexity of the tasks with which government must cope today, is very evident to the younger Irish politicians. Commenting on how politicians and the party are already affected by it, one official said:

> The business of government is so far beyond the ward committeemen and the local political leaders that they

can't cope with it. If you turn over the question of government to fifty aldermen, the city would bust within a month. They just couldn't do it. So these committeemen and the position more and more in a quiet, silent way is not what it used to be.

Who can figure out the financing on a bond issue, calculate the structure or the tensile strength of a piece of steel of twenty feet? Any ward committeeman? Or the fair market value of a piece of property on condemnation? Any alderman? The result, especially because Daley is where he is, is that the influence and power of ward committeemen is on the decline. We are sacrificing the party to government because government is too damned complex.

Such changes continually diminish the role of the party and, therefore, the access to government positions that Irish politicians have formerly claimed with little trouble. The "new" Irish politicians, therefore, appear to be the last wave of the Irish to have meaningful opportunities in government—even though they have been recruited as a "junior cadre"* by their Irish "elders," who hoped thereby to maintain the position of the Irish in the party or at least to fight an effective battle of political retreat.

Paralleling the changes in government and the party that have reduced the power of the Irish are the profound social, economic, and physical transformations that Chicago, like other urban centers, has undergone. Foremost among these is the continuing exodus of the middle class, especially couples with children, to the still burgeoning suburbs, a trend that includes more Irish every year. This metropolis has more than ever become the habitat of Negroes, Latin Americans, poor Southern whites, the anonymous and undifferentiated poor, and the middle and upper

---

* "There is no homework, but there are exams every hour. That's how the system works," according to one of the younger Irish politicians.

classes who reside in high-rise apartments, town house en-
claves, and socially inclusive communities. In the course
of the changing social composition of Chicago, some, like
the Negroes and the middle class, have either wrested more
political strength from the Irish by increasing their share
of public offices (as have the Negroes) or have been instrumental in affecting policy (as has the middle class).

Another reason why urban politics will be much less attractive to the Irish is that they have many better occupational opportunities elsewhere. Well represented among
the thousands of students who today are anxious about their
vocational futures without college training and credentials,
the Irish, now enrolling in nondenominational schools as
well as at Catholic educational institutions, have a steady
footing in the middle class. They find themselves much less
different and distant from the greater society, which their
predecessors really knew better as spectators rather than as
participants. Now the Irish have access to the great and expanding variety of jobs in industry, commerce, and the professions.

If the needs of a technological economy have helped or
obliged employers to overlook the diminishing social differences of prospective employees with marketable skills,
the Irish have also found society more receptive now that
religious differences have been muted. Events such as the
first Catholic-Episcopal rites held in Boston in 1964, with
the approval of Richard Cardinal Cushing, pointedly dram-
atize the change in mood among the Irish whose Catholicism is ever more similar to, but not yet identical with,
that of other Catholics. Then, too, the 1962 St. Patrick's
Day banquet of the Irish Fellowship Club held at Chicago's Conrad Hilton Hotel was, at twenty dollars a ticket,
at least as much a testimonial to mink stole and Florida
suntan affluence as to Irish achievement and solidarity.

Even though Irish ethnic identity is virtually crumbling for the younger generation, its influences are apt to be felt in politics for at least a few decades, and probably more than ever before in the suburban communities. The younger Irish who move there may have absorbed too much tradition to ignore or resist the tempting opportunities to seek elective office, even under nonpartisan arrangements. And reapportionment of the state assembly districts, which will give the metropolitan areas greater representation in the state capitols, may very well encourage the new Irish suburbanites to seek state offices, to which the Irish are by no means strangers.

The Irish have already become more attracted to national politics, which the Kennedy administration clothed with an unaccustomed aura of respectability and glamour. The excitement, humor, and style that the Kennedys introduced to Washington added much luster to both elective and administrative offices. In addition, service with the Peace Corps has drawn many Irish to its ranks; an Irish priest who examined a list of over six hundred Peace Corps members recently returned from two years of overseas service concluded that at least ten per cent of the returnees were unmistakably Irish.

Yet even as the Irish enter other political levels they will be in the process of losing their identity. They, as well as other ethnics, are increasingly being drawn into the amorphous middle class composed of Americans whose memories are individual and situational, whose problems include nearly everything but want, and whose color is drab. It is only a matter of decades before the Irish, and all other European groups, vanish into the "melting pot" that has only in recent years become more than an American fiction.

Appendix A:
Notes on Methodology

The author interviewed only those Irish politicians (non-Irish politicians were also interviewed) and priests both of whose parents were Irish. The purpose in so restricting the sample was to avoid the risk of having the evidence even partially distorted by those from slightly differing backgrounds. Parenthetically, it was observed that those of half-Irish parentage invariably identified with the Irish parent, a phenomenon best explained by the Irish parent's stronger commitment to Catholicism.

Next, all but four Irish politicians holding elective office in the city and county governments were interviewed. Those four preferred not to be interviewed. Furthermore, all but two committeemen were interviewed.

In addition, Irish politicians holding appointive office at all levels of the city and county governments, and a few in the state government, were randomly interviewed. Among this sample were many precinct captains. Information was also gathered from interviews and informal conversations in Irish neighborhoods and taverns, at Irish dances, and from Irish students at Illinois Institute of Technology and the University of Chicago.

The great majority of interviews with Irish politicians and priests ran over one hour, and approximately ten were interviewed a second time. A few others were willing to be interviewed as frequently as requested. A total of 93 separate interviews was conducted, and interviewing was terminated when those who were seen last were only able to reiterate what others had discussed.

Open-end interviews were used exclusively except for certain kinds of questions that sought brief, factual information. The reason for using this kind of interview exclusively was that it effectively draws out the nuances and subtleties more readily and much more thoroughly than can statistical analyses and survey questionnaires. Such interviews are also indispensable in opening new areas of thought to the researcher who will permit those being interviewed to explore their ruminations and "digressions," for these can scarcely be anticipated.

Appendix B:
Prototypical and Atypical Irish Politicians

The changes in social perspective and position of the Irish and Irish politicians can be traced through a biographical sketch of Mayor Richard J. Daley, who represents the link between the "old" and the "new" Irish politicians. His career is also compared with that of his predecessor, Mayor Martin H. Kennelly, to illustrate the differences between a "typical" and an "atypical" Irish politician.

Daley was born in Bridgeport, just a block away from his current residence (3536 South Lowe), which is not far from the stockyards where he worked as a boy to supplement a meager family income. He attended Catholic schools, enrolling at De LaSalle Institute when its student body was predominantly Irish (Mayors Kelly and Kennelly were also students there), and graduated with a law degree from De Paul University in Chicago's Loop.

Mayor Daley's political career is not only a most impressive one, but is the governmental counterpart of the once-lauded American "inner-directed" business tradition: the young man who began his career as a stock boy and, after wide and invaluable experience gained in the course of working his way up the company ladder, finally won recognition by being appointed president and chairman of the board. The offices, in the order in which Mayor Daley has held them, are: Secretary of the Chicago City Council (1925); Illinois State Representative (1936); Illinois State Senate (1938); Illinois State Director of Revenue (1949); Clerk of Cook County (1950); Chairman of the Cook County Central Committee (1953); and Mayor of Chicago (1955). Daley was also a precinct captain from 1924 until 1947, when he became committeeman of the Eleventh Ward Regular Democratic Organization, a position he continues to hold.

Daley lost only one election in his career—when he ran for the office of Sheriff of Cook County (1946), a position that is invariably a dead-end in Chicago Democratic politics. Apart from this incident, Daley sought and achieved the highest positions in both the municipal government and the party. The mayor, the prototypical product of the political party system, is very likely the most powerful politician Chicago has known.

Daley has remained in touch with those he has known longest and best, a few of whom he consults for their opinions on issues with which he must deal, and is still most at ease when chatting with fellow politicians. His immediate assistants at City Hall are usually other Irishmen from the Eleventh Ward whose families he has known for years. His expanded political and social interests have not altered the habits of a lifetime. Daley firmly believes that a strong Democratic party and Democratic administrations are the best assurances that Chicago's future, to which he is so consummately dedicated, will be one of great accomplishment and attractive change. Above all, he hopes to bequeath his family the reputation of having been responsible for Chicago's revitalization and its entering the ranks of the foremost cities of the world.

In having become the indisputable head of the Democratic party in the city and the most influential Democratic figure in county and state politics, Daley is nonetheless involved in a paradox. His current interests and ambitions necessarily incline him to seek status gratifications that have in the past been wholly atypical of both himself and of most other Irish politicians. Evidence of the inclusion of such interests (which involve a change in political style) is found in his having been listed as one of the ten best-dressed men in the country, and having been responsible for the State Department's placing Chicago on the scheduled tours of visiting foreign dignitaries. In 1959, Mayor Daley was host to the Queen of England, a gesture prompted by his strong personal interest in achieving status for both his city and himself.

Other status considerations that have become a standard part of his political activities include his frequent appearances at civic association banquets (where he is invariably accorded a standing applause upon his entry) and the formal cocktail parties that he periodically attends and at which he remains abstemious. The Mayor also serves as honorary chairman of such cultural enterprises as the Free Concerts Foundation and makes many speeches throughout the city at testimonials recognizing efforts of community leaders and the activities of community organizations. He formally honors the universities in the Chicago area, and acknowledges the contributions of their more celebrated faculty. As a result, he has acquired a degree of academic prestige, having been invited by out-of-state universities to address their students and faculty on political affairs.

Such status activities and interests have modified Daley's

political style. In recent years, for example, the Mayor rarely yields in public places or during interviews to his strong resentment of sharp criticism, justifiable or otherwise. Rather, he usually gives the impression of a calm, thoughtful, attentive, senior statesman patiently listening to the objections, and at times tawdry cavilling, of his critics and opponents.

It also appears that status considerations have absorbed Daley's time at the expense of important political matters and responsibilities. Informed persons have claimed that had Daley been as aware of party political affairs just a few years ago as he was in the past, he would have known of new power alignments within the party that would have precluded his conceding to Alderman Keane's (after Daley, the most powerful individual in the party) demand that either his brother or Seymour Simon be nominated by the party for the office of President of the Cook County Board of Commissioners. Nor does it seem likely that Daley would have misjudged the public's mood, had he been thoroughly engrossed in politics, when the six bond issues he recommended were defeated at a special referendum in 1962.

When he leaves public office (at this writing the signs suggest he will run for a fourth term), one can only wonder at how uneventful and colorless his life will be by comparison. Then, without governmental affairs to act as the bridge bringing him together with individuals with whom he normally does not socialize, he will have little, if any, social entrée to their leisure pastimes, civic activities, or business affairs. Of course, at his departure he will have left the party as strong as anyone could have expected in view of the shifting demographic patterns and the issues of race, education, taxes, and housing.

Martin H. Kennelly's entry into politics may very well be unique in the annals of Irish politics, for he had never held a party or governmental office prior to his nomination.

He had not, therefore, "earned" the nomination by rising in the ranks of the party. Moreover, he did not seek the office—he was sought by the party's Central Committee, which nominated him as its "blue ribbon" candidate to replace the incumbent Democratic Mayor Edward Kelly under whose administration graft and corruption had run rampant—"everybody had his snout in the trough."

Before becoming the party's nominee for mayor, Martin Kennelly was widely known and highly respected as a civic leader and an eminently successful businessman. He had headed Red Cross fund drives four times and had been president of the Warehouseman's National Association, president of the Traffic Club of Chicago, and vice president of the Chicago Association of Commerce and Industry. Kennelly had also been a member of the Industrial Advisory Committee of the Federal Reserve Bank of Chicago, and'had declined offers to serve unexpired terms as Sheriff of Cook County and State Director of Finance. As a prominent Roman Catholic layman, he had served as a trustee of De Paul University and board chairman of Holy Cross Hospital.

Kennelly's administration was chiefly noted for the following accomplishments: the expansion of civil service coverage; the establishment of an independent school board; the introduction of a general purchasing system; and the initiation of such urban renewal projects as the Lake Meadows apartment complex and the Congress Street Expressway.

Living at the Edgewater Beach Hotel, on Chicago's far northside, Kennelly was geographically, socially, and politically remote from party officials, politicians, and party workers. However, it could not have been otherwise given his background, which was responsible for his commitment to being an independent, business-minded, efficient mayor, a man who was expressly disinterested in the maintenance and control of the patronage system. What is more, Kennelly was so politically naive as to be unaware of the need to act assertively with the city council to have his policies confirmed. His failure to be an aggressive mayor enabled the city councilmen increasingly to ignore his wishes.

A number of those who knew him thought Kennelly was especially indecisive and that the party suffered from the emergence of factions which sought to fill the power vacuum he created. His inability and/or unwillingness to centralize power and strengthen the party led one Irish politician to say of Kennelly, "The people are entitled to more than an honest mayor." Another politician observed that "He'd rather have somebody else lead him than lead [others]."

No one could make such remarks about Daley, who has earned the respect and admiration, if not the affection, of politicians and bureaucrats. He has been instrumental in the revitalization and strengthening of the party, and is equally responsible for a relentless and forceful insistence upon administrative performance, if without equal concern for substantive considerations. Whatever his shortcomings, Daley has emerged as the strongest and most effective mayor and party chief Chicago and the Democratic party have ever known, and is, perhaps, the prototypical Irish politician.

Appendix C:
The Influence of Ethnicity on the Division of Political Labor

In sharp contrast to the Irish, there are men in Chicago's bureaucracy whose cultural and social experiences have so ill-prepared them for the uses of authority that they at once reveal their ethnicity by the rigid and awkward manner in which they comport themselves when conducting the duties of their positions. It seems more than conjectural that this figures among the reasons for their inability to claim the power in the party and patronage system to which their numbers in the city's population theoretically entitle them.

The influence of ethnic personality and cultural differences on the uses and interest in power is also notable in the curious division of political labor that has been struck upon by the Irish, Jews, and Protestants. The Irish are typically the tacticians and strategists, the organization

217

men, who assume responsibility for accepting and implementing the policy recommendations and data the others have devised or gathered for them. Taking note of this, an Irish politician remarked:

> You take _____ [Jewish] who works for me. He's the idea man and I'm responsible for making the policy work. He'll come up with an idea from time to time and get real excited about it, and I have to tell him from time to time that it just won't work. I have to be practical about it.

A comparable situation prevails in the mayor's office.

> You take Earl Bush. He's Jewish. He's Daley's public relations man. Whenever Daley makes a speech, who's the writer? Bush and no one else. . . . Now the public affairs men are Jack Reilly and Jim Kearney, they're in charge of conventions and other affairs like that. They're involved in doing things.

This division of labor was particularly evident on a higher level during the Kennedy campaign and administration. For example, President Kennedy's *political* brain trust included O'Donnell, O'Brien, Donahue, and Dungan, all Irishmen. His *personal* brain trust was composed of Sorenson, Goodwin, and Feldman, and his *academic* brain trust was staffed by Schlesinger, Galbraith, Bundy, and Rostow.[1] The differences in perspective between the Irish and hired professional staff were evident during election evening, 1960, when

> . . . Lou Harris worked his slide rule and attempted to sustain optimism by reading the totals in contrast to the Stevenson race of 1956; but downstairs, where the operational political chieftains—O'Brien, Donahue, and Dungan—received the reports they contrasted them with the Truman scores of 1948.[2]

The Reverend Joseph P. Fitzpatrick has found comparable differences between the Irish and Jews who were involved in the struggle to organize labor and to win better wages and working conditions for industrial workers. He has explained their divergent views concerning the broader question of social justice in terms of their religious experiences and substantiates the author's interpretation that the Irish stance on the important issues of the day has been determined by the religious issue. In his words:

> The American Labor Movement would not have been what it has been without Jews like Gompers, Strasser, Hillquit, Rosenberg, Hillman and Dubinsky; or without Irishmen like Powderly, Mitchell, Murray and Meany.
>
> However, in this effort the orientation of Jews was somewhat different from that of the Catholics. The Jews of the new migration had come from areas of Europe where socialism was the workingman's gospel. They reflected this in their zeal for reform, their activity in the labor movement, their attitude toward politics. Their energy and genius contributed a strong influence toward correcting injustices. But they were not interested in revolution for its own sake. When the traditional political organizations adopted many of the policies of the Socialists, the interest of the Jews in Socialism declined.
>
> This experience leaves the Jews with a liberal orientation toward social questions, politics and reform. They move with much confidence and ease in this kind of environment. They have been in and out of socialism; it was part of the family. They are not as likely to be alarmed over the presence of liberal, even radical forces.
>
> The orientation of Catholics was different. The Irish, particularly, had experienced two centuries of desperate struggle against oppression. They had been through a long and bitter schooling in the fight for freedom and justice. But the focus of revolutionary efforts was mainly in the freedom of their faith. The radicalism of the Irish was religiously oriented. In fact, one thing that confused the Irish efforts toward freedom and justice in their early days in the

United States was the fact that radical movements here tended to be irreligious if not anti-religious.

. . . .

. . . Catholics define a secularist orientation as a threat to religious freedom; Jews define it as the protection of religious freedom. Thus the same central ideal of American life is approached through two different orientations.[3]

As assimilation has overtaken both the Irish and the Jews, eroding their social characteristics and obliterating much of their identities, this division of labor tends to disappear. This change is especially notable as devout young Irish Catholics have moved into the forefront of the civil rights movement passing, as it were, those young middle-class Jews who have discarded their parents' political orientation and become staunchly conservative Republicans, adherents of laissez-faire economics and government, and disenchanted with the advocates and objectives of civil rights.

Notes

Notes to Chapter 2

1. Edmund Curtis, *A History of Ireland,* 3d ed. (New York: Barnes and Noble, 1937), p. 168.

2. *Ibid.,* pp. 165-6.

3. *Ibid.,* pp. 251, 254.

4. Edward MacLysaght, *Irish Life in the Seventeenth Century,* 2d ed. (Dublin: Cork University Press, 1950), p. 295.

5. Alexander M. Sullivan, *New Ireland* (London: S. Low, Marston, Searle, and Rivington, 1878), p. 79.

6. George Creel, *Ireland's Fight for Freedom* (New York: Harper, 1919), p. 111.

7. John P. Gannon, *A Review of Irish History* (London: T. Fisher-Unwin, 1900), p. 276.

8. Curtis, *op. cit.,* p. 117.

9. George M. Potter, *To the Golden Door* (Boston: Little, Brown and Co., 1960), p. 40.

10. R. Barry O'Brien, ed., *Two Centuries of Irish History: 1691-1870,* 2d ed. (London: Paul, Trench, Trubner and Co., Ltd., 1907), xx. Cf. Potter, *op cit.,* p. 41.

11. Robert B. McDowell, *Irish Public Opinion: 1750-1800* (London: Faber and Faber, 1944), p. 33. The following makes more

vivid the distressing conditions of the Irish due to the greed and callousness of their landlords:

"Rents, fixed by competitive proposals from the prospective tenants rather than on a valuation of the land, tended to be high. Naturally many tenants found themselves unable or unwilling to pay the rent so fixed, and every year a number of ejections took place and distresses were levied—the latter being a wasteful and embittering way of recovering arrears by a seizure of the tenant's crops and possessions. Legally it was usually easy to get rid of a tenant, for the great bulk of the occupying tenants held at will, which in practice meant on a yearly tenancy, so that insecurity—with its inevitable concomitants, inertia, improvidence and untidiness—was a distressing feature of Irish peasant life." R. B. McDowell, "Ireland on the Eve of the Famine," in R. D. Edwards and T. D. Williams, eds., *The Great Famine* (New York: New York University Press, 1957), pp. 8-9.

"The landlord was not, as in England, a partner in agricultural production, investing capital in fencing, drainage, farmhouses, and cottages, and bound to the cultivator by social and prescriptive ties, but simply the receiver of a rent-charge." J. H. Bridges, "From the Union to Catholic Emancipation," in O'Brien, *op. cit.*, p. 206. Cf. also pp. 208, 211.

12. Sean O'Faolain, *The Irish* (New York: Devin-Adair Co., 1949), p. 131.

13. Gustave de Beaumont, "Ireland: Social, Political, and Religious," in James Carty, *Ireland:1783-1850* (Dublin: C. J. Fallon, 1949), p. 110.

14. Rev. James Gordon, *A History of the Rebellion in Ireland* (London: J. Dewick, 1808), p. 148. Rev. Gordon, an Ulster Protestant, makes the point that the priests' leadership roles were a function of their closeness to and dependence upon the people. "The almost total dependence of the clergy of Ireland upon their people for the means of subsistence, is the cause, according to my best judgment, why upon every popular commotion many priests of that communion have been . . . [and] always will be found in the ranks of sedition and opposition to the established government." *See also*, p. 342.

15. Thomas Sugrue, *A Catholic Speaks His Mind* (New York: Harper, 1951), p. 45.

16. Curtis, *op. cit.*, p. 333.

17. McDowell, *op. cit.*, p. 178.

18. Dennis Gwynn, Young Ireland and 1848 (Cork, Ireland: Cork University Press, 1949), p. 234.

19. William E. Gladstone, quoted in Carty, *op. cit.*, p. 45.

20. Curtis, *op. cit.*, p. 222.

21. W. H. Lecky, *History of Ireland in the Eighteenth Century*, in James Carty, ed., *Ireland: 1783-1850* (Dublin: C. J. Fallon, 1949), p. 101.

22. Potter, *op. cit.*, pp. 45-6.

23. *Ibid.*, pp. 53-4. Among other accounts of the violence and lawlessness which were the general conditions among the Irish because of agrarian oppression, cf. R. Barry O'Brien, *op. cit.*, pp. xxix, xxx, and Curtis, *op. cit.*, p. 317.

24. M. McDonnell Bodkin, *Recollections of an Irish Judge* (New York: Dodd, Mead, and Co. 1915), p. 159.

25. Potter, *op. cit.*, pp. 63-4.

Arensberg described the functions of favor, interest, and influence as follows: ". . . the countryman expected favours for favours rendered. He knew best the direct and personal approaches of social obligation. So, at first, geese and country produce besieged the new officers and magistrates; a favourable decision or a necessary public work performed was interpreted as a favour given. It demanded a direct and personal return. 'Influence' to the countryman was and is a direct personal relationship, like the friendship of the countryside along which his life moves. Like money, 'influence' was a somewhat mysterious entity; it seemed to be a powerful agent for both good and evil. But its real content seemed understandable enough; it was an easily recognizable social bond." Conrad Arensberg, *The Irish Country-Man: An Anthropological Study* (New York: MacMillan, 1937), p. 178. Cf. also pp. 175-6.

Referring to the relationship of factions to the dispensation of justice, Bridges wrote: "Shanavats and Caravats, Coffees, and Rieckavollos, and the other factions whose quarrels bedinned the country-side, had each their own protecting magistrate, to whom they paid blackmail in the shape of labor. 'A word in the court was better than a pound in the purse.' " Bridges, in Bryce, *op. cit.*, p. 219.

26. In fact the Irish won very little real political gains through this Act. As Bridges has pointed out, "the status of the Catholics, who numbered, perhaps, four-fifths of the total population, was left very incomplete by the enfranchising Act of 1793. A Catholic could not be a member of Parliament, nor a judge, nor attorney-general or solicitor-general, nor a king's counsel, nor a privy councillor. He

could not be a mayor, alderman, or a common councilman of any corporation [city]; nor could he hold a fellowship in Trinity College. To other offices he was admissible, but from most he was in practice excluded. There were, in 1826, eighteen public magistrates in Dublin; not one was a Catholic. There were seven hundred and sixty-four offices, great and small, connected with the medical and charitable institutions of the city; Catholics held thirty-three of these. Of four hundred and thirty-six appointments in the Excise and Customs, they held eighteen. Of more than two thousand offices connected with the administration of justice, not more than thirty-nine had been entrusted to them. The power of voting at elections was an important gain. *But so far as the peasantry were concerned, this right remained practically in abeyance for thirty years.*" (Emphasis added.) Bridges, in James Bryce, ed., *Two Centuries of Irish History* (London: Kegan, Paul, Trench and Co., 1888), p. 220.

27. *Ibid.,* p. 297.

28. Head's "Fortnight in Ireland," quoted in O'Brien, *op. cit.,* p. 442. In justification of the influence of the priests, ". . . it was eloquently urged by Plunket that, when law had mixed politics and religion together, the priesthood of Ireland were not to be condemned for calling attention to the principles of those who were likely to represent them. Had they not the right to say to their parishioners, 'Here is a man wishing to go into Parliament, who will there vituperate you, who will describe you as idolators, and who will oppose the attainment of your just rights'?" *Ibid.,* p. 303.

29. Henry Grattan, "Speech Against the Act of Union," in Carty, *op. cit.,* p. 52.

"The Irish parliament was compelled to legislate through an inconvenient and undignified procedure. The head of the Irish executive was an English lord lieutenant appointed on the advice of the English ministry. And Englishmen secured a large share of the profits, places, pensions, and sinecures pertaining to the Irish governmental machine." McDowell, *op. cit.,* p. 16.

30. McDowell, *op. cit.,* pp. 26-7. Cf. also p. 28.

31. Mrs. S. C. (Anna Maria) Hall, "Going to Law," *Stories of the Irish Peasantry* (Edinburgh: Wm. and Robert Chambers, 1851), p. 218.

32. Hall, "Do You Think I'd Inform," *ibid.,* p. 42.

33. William Carleton, "Traits and Stories of the Irish Peasantry," D. J. O'Donoghue, ed. *The Life of William Carleton* (London: Downey and Co., 1896), p. 46.

34. J. H. Bridges, "From the Union to Catholic Emancipation," in O'Brien, *op. cit.*, pp. 279-80.

35. *Ibid.*, pp. 298-9.

36. Rev. Patrick Rogers, "Catholic Emancipation," in Michael Tierney, ed., *Daniel O'Connell* (Dublin: Richview Press, 1949), pp. 136-7.

37. Potter, *op. cit.*, pp. 108-9.

38. Comment of Major Warburton, quoted from Wyse, *History of the Catholic Association*, Vol. I, by Bridges, *op. cit.*, in O'Brien, *op. cit.*, p. 281.

39. Lord Fitzmaurice and James R. Thursfield, "From the Emancipation of the Catholics to the Insurrectionary Movement of 1848," in O'Brien, *op. cit.*, p. 341.

40. De Beaumont, *op. cit.*, pp. 109-10.

Notes to Chapter 3

1. Cecil Woodham-Smith, "Ireland's Hunger, England's Fault?" *Atlantic Monthly*, January 1963, pp. 70-71.

2. *Ibid.*, p. 68.

3. Fitzmaurice and Thursfield, *op. cit.*, in O'Brien, *op. cit.*, p. 492.

4. Arnold Schrier, *Ireland and the American Emigration: 1850-1900* (Minneapolis: University of Minnesota Press, 1958), p. 53.

5. *Ibid.*, p. 52.

6. For an analysis of how excessive drinking impeded the economic mobility of the Irish, see Daniel Moynihan, "The Irish of New York," *Commentary*, August 1963, p. 100.

7. Will Herberg, "Religion and Culture in Present-Day America," in Thomas T. McAvoy, C.S.C., *Roman Catholicism and the American Way of Life* (Notre Dame: University of Notre Dame Press, 1960), p. 7.

8. Leonard Wibberly, *The Coming of the Green* (New York: Holt, 1958), p. 163.

9. *Ibid.*

10. Quoted from *Cincinnati Catholic Telegraph*, February 6, 1845, by Willard E. Wight, "The Native American Catholic, and Immigrant, and the Immigration," *op. cit.*, p. 212.

11. Oscar Handlin, *Boston's Immigrants* (Cambridge: Harvard University Press, 1959), p. 127.

Notes to Chapter 4

1. Milton M. Gordon, "Assimilation in America," *Daedalus*, Spring, 1961, p. 279.

2. *Ibid.*

3. *Ibid.*

4. Ruth M. Piper, *The Irish in Chicago* (Unpublished master's thesis, Department of Political Science, University of Chicago), p. 37.

5. Schrier, *op. cit.*, pp. 63-4.

6. Thomas Sugrue, *A Catholic Speaks His Mind* (New York: Harper, 1959), p. 45.

7. John Tracy Ellis, *Perspectives in American Catholicism* (Baltimore: Helicon, 1963), p. 61.

8. *Ibid.*

9. Wibberly, *op. cit.*, pp. 136-7.

The general reluctance of the clergy to come to the aid of the labor movement is evidenced by the following: "The attitude of the Catholic clergy can not be [as] clearly defined [as that of the Irish in the labor] movement. . . . Some prominent Catholics, including Irish labor leaders like Terrence Vincent Powderly, have asserted that the clergy did not enter the fight for social justice till the victory was practically won." Carl Wittke, *We Who Built America* (New York: Prentice-Hall, 1940), p. 219.

10. John A. Ryan, *Social Doctrine in Action* (New York: Harper & Brothers, 1941), p. 96.

11. John F. Maguire, *The Irish in America* (London: Longmans, Green & Co., 1868), p. 533.

12. *Ibid.*, p. 277.

13. James P. Shannon, "The Irish Catholic Emigration," in Thomas T. McAvoy, C. S. C. ed., *Roman Catholicism and the American Way of Life* (Notre Dame: University of Notre Dame Press, 1960), p. 208.

14. The relationship between the priests and the people remains very close even today, although with less binding force than in the early 1890's when a dispute between a parish priest, Father Edward McGlynn, and Archbishop Michael Corrigan over the former's public advocacy of the single tax led to his temporary excommunication. Prior to his reinstatement somewhat afterwards ". . . thousands left the Church [and] there are Protestant families in [this] town today which were Catholic until this episode." Sugrue, *op. cit.*, p. 44.

15. G. P. MacDonnell, "From the Insurrectionary Movement of 1848 to the Land Act of 1870," in O'Brien, *op. cit.*, p. 441.

The following is further evidence of the Church's unwillingness to permit the Irish to attend non-Catholic educational institutions. "Peel proposed and founded in 1849 what came to be known as Queen's Colleges. They were non-denominational, under secular control, and no provision was made for teaching philosophy or history according to Catholic viewpoints. The younger idealists and rebels (the Young Irelanders) would have welcomed any scheme which would have provided higher education for the people; the bishops . . . rejected it; and when the scheme developed in spite of them the bishops laboured to keep the middle-classes from sending their children to these Queen's Colleges." Sean O'Faolain, *The Irish* (New York: Devin-Adair, 1949), p. 141.

16. Robert Considine, *It's the Irish* (New York: Doubleday & Co., 1961), pp. 107-8.

17. John Tracy Ellis, *American Catholicism* (Chicago: University of Chicago Press, 1956), p. 102.

18. The authority of the priests and nuns in disciplinary matters is discussed in greater detail in Chapter 7. However, the following excerpt from James T. Farrell's, *My Days of Anger,* quite explicitly makes the point that the Irish expected their youngsters to comply fully with the authority of the priests:

"Uncle Al came in . . .
'Say, what the hell is this goddamned business, your getting kicked out of school, talking back to the priest?'
Bob looked at his uncle, afraid.
'Listen, when I talk to you, answer me.'
'I only stood up for my rights.'
'Why, you goddamned little fool, aren't you ashamed of yourself.' "
James T. Farrell, *My Days of Anger* (New York: Popular Library, 1943), p. 280.

19. Fishman makes this same point, if in a different, though related, context: ". . . the issue of self-directed separation versus greater integration in the American community is a live one among Catholics, with both alternatives actively competing. Unlike the Jewish community, there are no structurally safeguarded gradational subdivisions within the Catholic religious leadership that correspond to alternative retentivistic philosophies." Joshua A. Fishman, "Childhood Indoctrination," *Daedalus,* Spring 1961, p. 335.

It is well to remember that Irish Catholicism was very slow to develop a diversity of religious and secular perspectives because the Irish who held the most respected authority roles, the clergy and politicians, shared a fairly uniform outlook toward Protestant society whose ideological and social variety they could not adopt while the religious cleavage interdicted meaningful social interaction among them.

20. O'Faolin, *op. cit.*, p. 138.

The power of the clergy over education is confirmed by the following: "Orestes Brownson [an American convert to Catholicism] trembled not so much at the possible infection of the Catholic Irish by intellectual interests as their want of intellectual interests of any kind, though influential clergymen argued in justification of the lack of intellectual curiosity among the Irish." Potter, *op. cit.*, p. 606.

21. Finley Peter Dunne, *Mr. Dooley: On Making a Will and Other Necessary Evils* (New York: Charles Scribner's Sons, 1919), p. 24.

22. Dunne, *Mr. Dooley's Opinions* (New York: R. H. Russell, 1901), p. 203. Mr. Dooley also had the following to say about the importance of a college education:

"What's a degree, says ye? A degree is a certyficate fr'm a ladin' university entitlin' ye to wear a Mother Hubbard in spite iv th' polis. It makes ye a doctor iv something an' enables ye to practise at ye'er profission. I don't mind tellin' ye, Hinnissy, that if I was a law, which I'm not, I'd have to be pretty sick before I'd call in manny iv th' doctors iv laws I know, an' as f'r American lithrachoor, it don't need a doctor so much as a coroner. But annyhow degrees is good things because they livils all ranks. . . . Some iv th' thriftier univarsities is makin' a degree th' alternytive iv a fine. Five dollars or docthor iv laws." *Ibid.*, pp. 202-3.

23. James T. Farrell, "All Things Are Nothing to Me," in *The Short Stories of James T. Farrell* (New York: Penguin Books, 1946), p. 151.

24. Quoted in Oscar Handlin, *Boston's Immigrants* (Cambridge: Harvard University Press, 1959), p. 176.

25. Maguire, *op. cit.*, p. 447.

26. *Boston Pilot*, July 29, 1854, quoted in Willard E. Wight, "The Native American Catholic, the Immigrant, and Immigration," in Thomas T. McAvoy C.S.C. ed., *Roman Catholicism and the American Way of Life* (Notre Dame: Notre Dame University Press, 1960), p. 214.

27. Potter, *op. cit.*, p. 276.

28. Handlin, *op. cit.*, p. 198.

"The Hibernian crusade against liquor . . . in its later manifestations . . . was definitely and uncompromisingly Catholic, with
emphasis on prayer, sacraments, and supernatural help, and there
was to be no fraternization with temperance movements in which
Protestants were prominent." Wittke, *op. cit.*, p. 50. See also p. 49.

29. Ryan, *op. cit.*, p. 96.

30. Wittke, *op. cit.*, pp. 129-30.

31. Wibberly, *op. cit.*, p. 54.

Potter offers the following analysis of the Irish view of the reformers' drive to abolish slavery:

"It should be remarked . . . that Catholic Irish opinion, except in
the drive for political equality, in which it was radical in temper and
method, was more likely than not to be found on the conservative
side. The Irishman by nature as well as by the teachings of his
Church, opposed innovations, had little patience with reform and
reformers, and put small faith in the use of law to change or perfect
human beings. The leading Catholic Irish lawyers upheld the strict
construction of the Constitution on slavery, in this being at one with
the conservative legal minds of the North.

The *Boston Pilot* in 1839 urged its Catholic readers to beware of
the danger of contributing, even in the smallest degree, to the support of abolitionist and antislavery societies: "That we should simply
caution our fellow Catholics to stand aloof from these insidious and
bloody-minded sectarians is not enough. We charge them with
treason to the country—as conspirators against the peace of society—
and as a class of tyrants of the most dangerous and treacherous
character." Potter, *op. cit.*, p. 376. See also p. 374.

32. "Official Catholic doctrine held that slavery was not necessarily evil; it taught that slavery, thought of theoretically and apart
from specific abuses to human dignity, was not opposed to the divine
or natural law. Manumission was encouraged wherever circumstances would permit the slave to better his condition, and strong
emphasis was always placed on the moral obligation of Catholic
slaveholders to treat their subjects with justice and charity and to
see that they received religious instruction. Moreover, the Church's
condemnation of the slave trade was definite, something that had
been reiterated more than once, and as recently as December 1839,
in the apostolic letter of Pope Gregory XVI." John Tracy Ellis,
American Catholicism (Chicago: University of Chicago Press, 1956),
p. 87.

33. Wittke, *op. cit.*, p. 168.

34. "Perhaps the most interesting aspect of the history of the Irish Fortyeighters [an insurrectionary group] was the conflict between a small, radical minority and the Roman Catholic hierarchy. Meagher, for example, who considered himself a liberal Catholic and approved a nonsectarian educational system, was denounced as a 'red republican.' Furthermore, a large section of the American Catholic press disapproved of his sympathy for Kossuth and Mazzini." Wittke, *op. cit.*, p. 85.

35. Handlin, *op. cit.*, p. 138.

36. Lucian Pye, *Politics, Personality, and Nation Building* (New Haven: Yale University Press, 1962), p. 255.

37. Thomas F. O'Dea, *American Catholic Dilemma* (New York: Sheed and Ward, 1958), pp. 89-9, 40, 78-9.

NOTES TO CHAPTER 5

1. Cf. Samuel Lubell, *The Future of American Politics* (New York: Harper and Brothers, 1951), Ch. 7. "The [Chicago] Irish . . . declined significantly in their Democratic support [from 1948 to 1956 in presidential elections]. When the various Irish precincts were isolated and ranked according to median years of education in 1950, it was found that the higher educated precincts were significantly lower in their Democratic support than the less educated Irish precincts. In addition, the Irish precincts generally exhibited voting behavior similar to Republican blocs when voting on 'money spending' issues in special proposition contests." R. Gene Geisler, *Chicago Democratic Voting: 1947-57* (Unpublished dissertation, University of Chicago), p. 154.

2. Cf. Potter, *op. cit.*, p. 219.

3. Wibberly, *op. cit.*, p. 47.

4. Edward A. Shils, "Authoritarianism 'Right' and 'Left.'" in Richard Christie and Marie Jahoda, eds., *Studies in the Scope and Method of "The Authoritarian Personality"* (Glencoe: Free Press, 1954), p. 42.

5. Wittke, *op. cit.*, p. 165. According to Roberts, "from their first appearance in the cities in large numbers, the Irish were largely in control of the saloon business *with its important relationship to politics*. The . . . Irish masters and bartenders of these gathering places were important links in the chain of political organization.

The saloons were further utilized by the masters of the machine in the dispensation of that broad charity which was one of their most powerful instruments in controlling the votes of the humbler and more indigent members of society." (Emphasis added.) Edward F. Roberts, *Ireland in America* (New York: Prentice-Hall, 1940), p. 127.

6. Arensberg, *op. cit.*, p. 178.

7. Considine, *op. cit.*, pp. 110-11.

8. For a colorful account of how the police and thugs were employed to prevent opponents of the ward organization from entering the polls when Kenna and Coughlin controlled Chicago's First Ward, see Lloyd Wendt and Herman Kogan, *Lords of the Levee* (New York: Bobbs-Merrill, 1943).

9. Wibberly, *op. cit.*, p. 173.

10. Nathan Glazer and Daniel P. Moynihan, *Beyond the Melting Pot* (Cambridge: The M.I.T. Press, 1964), p. 226.

11. Oscar Handlin, *Al Smith and His America* (Boston: Little, Brown and Co., 1958), pp. 19-20.

12. Pye, *op. cit.*, p. 5.

13. Edward A. Ross, *The Old World in the New* (New York: The Century Co., 1914), p. 261.

A confirming observation has been made by Shannon, who says: "The whole idea that one would lose an election for the sake of any abstract principle is alien to [the] Irish tradition. Equally alien is the notion that the interests of the present generation should be sacrificed for the sake of some future benefit." William V. Shannon, *The American Irish* (New York: The MacMillan Co., 1963), p. 402.

14. James T. Farrell, *My Days of Anger* (New York: Popular Library, 1961), p. 123.

15. William L. Riordon, *Plunkitt of Tammany Hall* (New York: Knopf, 1948), viii.

16. Potter, *op. cit.*, p. 229.

Mr. Dooley made the same point somewhat differently, saying:

"Out here [Chicago] a man that often changes his shirt don't often change his pollytics. A man's in th' same party till he take th' broad jump—an' sometimes aftherward, f'r most iv th' people in this ward wud die befure they'd be burrid by a raypublican undertaker." Finley Peter Dunne, *Mr. Dooley's Opinions* (New York: R. H. Russell, 1901), pp. 171-2.

Pye places the same sentiment in a theoretical context: "The communal framework also sharply limits freedom in altering political allegiances. Any change in political identification generally requires a change in one's social and personal relationships; conversely, any change in social relations tends to result in a change in political identification." Pye, *op. cit.*, p. 17.

17. Joseph Roddy, "After Nudity, What?" *Look*, March 9, 1965.

NOTES TO CHAPTER 6

1. *Chicago Tribune*, March 8, 1951.

2. Carter H. Harrison, *Stormy Years* (New York: Bobbs-Merrill Co., 1935), pp. 78-9.

3. Cf. Alex Gottfried, *Boss Cermak* (Seattle: University of Washington Press, 1962), p. 175.

4. Shannon, in an observation about President Kennedy, confirms the contention that the Irish have characteristically considered politics as a career.

"Although he had studied briefly under Professor Harold Laski and had studied under some liberal professors at Harvard, [President Kennedy] did not enter politics with any youthful radical convictions. He entered politics in a *typical Irish way:* It was a profession in which a man could build a career." Shannon, *op. cit.*, p. 398. (Emphasis added.)

5. When Anton Cermak won control of the party and the nomination for mayor in 1931, the Irish were obviously displeased.

"It was clear that Thompson [the incumbent Republican] fell heir to a sizable vote from the Irish and from wards controlled by Irish leaders. Although most of the Irish leaders delivered their wards to the Czech candidate, only one of the wards delivering best for Cermak had an Irish boss; and this boss was A. J.'s old friend, McDonough. Of the four wards which Cermak carried by less than a thousand votes, all had Irish bosses: Igoe, Moran, Walsh, and Touhy.

Of the wards in which Cermak's majority was relatively small (no more than seven to five), the overwhelming number were controlled by Irish bosses: Whalen, Powers, O'Toole, Layden, Noonan, Brady, Bowler [not Irish], Clark, Kelly, T. J. Crowe, Gill and Donahue. Only three wards controlled by non-Irish leaders belong to this category: those of Kohl, Jensen and Pryzbylo. Of these, Kohl was a T. J. Crowe-Clark man. It should be noted however, that the wards of these Irish leaders had either been carried by Thompson in 1927 or, in those cases where Dever [the defeated Democratic nominee whose nomination the Irish had opposed] had won, had given Dever a smaller vote than was given to Cermak. Some of them had also given Thompson some of his greatest pluralities in the 1931 primary. . . . In sum, it seems quite likely that the Irish ward leaders had not exercised all their muscle in order to increase the majority of the Czech candidate." Gottfried, *op. cit.*, pp. 236-7.

6. While it seems reasonable that family reputation has had the same relevance for recruiting of Irish politicians in other cities where they have been in politics, the following, from Flynn's autobiography, indicates its importance among the Irish in New York City politics:

"I am certain that [I was] selected [as the Democratic nominee in the Second Assembly District in New York], not because of anything I stood for, nor because of any personal strength I might bring to the party, but because of my father's good name and my brother's wide acquaintance and high standing in the district." Edward J. Flynn, *You're the Boss* (New York: Viking Press, 1947), p. 12.

The author's argument is that family reputation is unique to the Irish as a *group*, not that it is unknown among other individuals. For example, had Adlai Stevenson III been Tom Jones and Milton Eisenhower been Manuel Gonzalez they would probably have scored less notable election victories than they did in Illinois' last (and *at large*) state assembly election, when each outran all other candidates in his respective party.

7. Peter B. Clark, *The Big Businessman as a Civic Leader* (unpublished dissertation, Department of Political Science, University of Chicago), p. 82.

8. Moynihan makes the same point about the Irish politicians in New York:

"The liberals are people with what is called a high rate of upward mobility. Not so the regulars, who incline to stay near the old neighborhoods, speaking with the old accents, even after they have become rich and successful. This makes for different views of what constitutes proper conduct in the political game. To be upwardly mobile means to be successfully aggressive—a preeminent trait of liberals, for all that their aggressiveness tends to be of the sophisticated variety. The regulars generally view such liberals as persons without enough manners to wait their turn." Daniel Moynihan, " 'Bosses' and 'Reformers'," *Commentary*, June 1961, p. 464.

9. Riordon, *op. cit.*, pp. 10-11. See also pp. 69-70.

The ingrained reticence of Irish politicians, which is especially noticeable in those who move to positions of power, has found expression in Irish literature. The following excerpt is from *The Last Hurrah*.

"Skeffington, who understood his people thoroughly, knew their virtually bottomless capacity for suspicion and ridicule; and had seen other leaders, popular men all, who when suddenly suspected of pretension, of getting a bit above themselves, had been turned on with a savagery which could scarcely be believed. The trick was, he knew, to space the grand phrases properly, to use them always with the air of winking complicity; to suggest, in other words, of allowable erudition untinted by the dangerous streaks of self-inflation." O'Connor, *op. cit.*, p. 9.

10. An Irish politician discussing the relationship of Catholicism to the Irish understanding of politics stated:

"This question is a problem that involves people who are idealists. One of their traits—usually they're without roots, they have parental difficulties, or are agnostic or atheistic. It's because they have no religious or philosophical background. Everything with them is finite. They're seeking the millenium tomorrow—they don't take into account or put into proper perspective man's frailty, man as a creature who can err. People are going to have bad days and good days. We all suffer for our frailties, for greed and pride. I think a person who has a philosophical or religious background recognizes these are a part of the human race and realizes no matter what happens that these traits are always with us. A person goes off the deep end if he doesn't recognize man's shortcomings and the futility of attaining ideals. You've got to recognize that he's susceptible to human vice."

More general confirmation of this point is given by Shannon who states: "Perfection in politics, it has been said, is a Protestant vision. . . . General Eisenhower demonstrated this in 1952 when he characterized what was, after all, just another partisan campaign as a 'moral crusade.' No Catholic politician who understood his own religious philosophy could make such a claim." Shannon, *op. cit.*, p. 403.

11. If honoured more in the breach than in observation in some societies, and probably least characteristic of middle-class politics, "loyalty is an absolute value in all forms of politics, but it is peculiarly basic to traditional systems in which men are moved by the sentiments of personal association and by an understanding of the ap-

propriateness of rewards for services rendered. Under such circumstances loyalty [becomes] honesty, and both [can] give a degree of predictability to human relationships." Pye, *op. cit.*, p. 69.

12. "In part, the stress on the affective or expressive aspect of politics is related to the fact that . . . questions of personal loyalties and identification are recognized as providing the basic issues of politics and the bond between leader and follower is generally an emotional one. In fact, in many non-Western societies it is considered highly improper and even immoral for people to make loyalty contingent upon their leaders' ability to solve the problems of public policy." *Ibid.*, p. 29.

13. Potter, *op. cit.*, p. 237.

14. Riordon, *op. cit.*, pp. 47-8.

15. Personal loyalty was just as important to Senator Edward Kennedy during the period when he was lining up support for his campaign. "One state senator reported that he was in Teddy's camp because Teddy told him flatly 'You are either for me or against me. No neutrals are allowed.'" *USA*°1, May, 1962, p. 26.

16. Glazer and Moynihan, *op. cit.*, p. 229.

17. This standard is of such importance to the Irish that, as with other vital aspects of their life, it has found its way into Irish literature. O'Connor depicts marital infidelity as so heinous a sin as to drive an Irish woman to divorce, itself an extraordinarily sinful act among the Irish.

"'They'll turn on you,' Skeffington said inexorably, 'because *you've done the one thing you can't do with our people and get away with it.* You're a married man who's been fooling around with another woman, Johnnie, and it's all going to come out. Your wife is going to divorce you. . . . I know she's been to see Father Casey, and I know that no matter what he or anybody else says—least of all you, Johnnie—she's fed up and she's going to sue for a civil divorce. And you know what'll happen when the word gets out. They'll [the Irish voters] repudiate you so fast you won't be able to catch your breath.'" O'Connor, *op. cit.*, pp. 208-9.

18. The Sixty-First Annual Banquet of the Irish Fellowship Club of Chicago (St. Patrick's Day, 1962) was an event of such importance as to have Mayors Richard Daley and Robert Briscoe (Dublin, Ireland) as its main speakers. The Irish notables seated at the speakers table included 29 politicians, 8 priests and 12 businessmen. Of the nineteen members of the Arrangement Committee, 11

were in politics. Of the sixty-one past presidents, 33 had held some elective or appointive political position. A musical program of all-Irish tunes was performed by Lou Breese and his orchestra.

19. Fr. Joseph H. Fichter, *Parochial School: A Sociological Analysis* (Notre Dame: Notre Dame University Press, 1958), p. 39.

NOTES TO APPENDIX C

1. These categorical distinctions are found in Theodore H. White, *The Making of the President* (New York: Atheneum Publishers, 1961), p. 284.

2. *Ibid.*, p. 21.

3. Rev. Joseph P. Fitzpatrick, "Catholic and Jew in Urban Life," *Chicago Sun-Times*, June 18, 1961.

Index

AF